M000078598

CREED

CREED

A SEVEN-WEEK REFLECTION GUIDE
ON THE APOSTLES' CREED

J. D. WALT

Copyright 2012 by Seedbed Publishing

All rights reserved. No portion of this book may be reproduced, stored in a retrieval system, or transmitted in any form or by any means—electronic, mechanical, photocopy, recording, scanning, or other— except for brief quotations in critical reviews or articles, without the prior written permission of the publisher.

All scripture quotations, unless otherwise indicated, are taken from THE HOLY BIBLE, NEW INTERNATIONAL VERSION®. Copyright © 1973, 1978, 1984 by International Bible Society. Used by permission of Zondervan. All rights reserved.

Scripture quotations marked NIV are taken from THE HOLY BIBLE, NEW INTERNATIONAL VERSION®, NIV® Copyright © 1973, 1978, 1984, 2011 by Biblica, Inc.™ Used by permission. All rights reserved worldwide.

Printed in the United States of America

Library of Congress Control Number: 2012946253

Paperback ISBN: 978-1-62824-000-9
Mobipocket ISBN: 978-1-62824-001-6
ePub ISBN: 978-1-62824-002-3
uPDF ISBN: 978-1-62824-003-0

Cover and page design by Haley Hill

SEEDBED PUBLISHING
Sowing for a Great Awakening
204 N. Lexington Avenue, Wilmore, Kentucky 40390
www.seedbed.com

Contents

Week 3:
Who Was Conceived by the Holy Spirit, Born of the Virgin Mary, Suffered under Pontius Pilate; Was Crucified, Died and Was Buried

Week 4:
He Descended to the Dead. The Third Day He Arose from the Dead. He Ascended into Heaven and Sits at the Right Hand of God the Father Almighty. From There, He Shall Come to Judge the Living and the Dead

Week 5:
I Believe in the Holy Spirit

Contents

Week 6:
The Holy Catholic Church, the Communion of Saints

Week 7:
The Forgiveness of Sins, the Resurrection of the Body, and the Life Everlasting

About the Author

Christian Symbols

Alpha and Omega

In Revelation 1:8, the Lord said, "I am the Alpha and the Omega; who is and who was and who is to come, the Almighty." This symbol captures the comprehensive nature of the reign of Jesus Christ.

Descending Dove

The descending dove symbolizes the descent of the Holy Spirit at the baptism of Jesus as described in all four Gospels. It also often references the descent of the Holy Spirit on the Day of Pentecost.

Ichthus

In Greek, *ichthus* (ΙΧΘΥΣ), the word for fish, serves also as an acronym "Jesus Christ, God's Son, Savior." Early Christians, fearful of persecution, identified themselves to one another with this secret symbol from the late second century.

INRI

INRI is the Latin inscription over the cross. The letters stand for "Jesus of Nazarenus Rex Iudaiorum," which translates to "Jesus of Nazareth, King of the Jews."

Agnus Dei

The Lamb of God, carrying the Banner of Victory. The banner itself is sometimes called the Easter or Resurrection Banner, symbolizing Christ's victory over death. The three-rayed halo signifies divinity. In John 1:29, we read that when John the Baptist saw Jesus, he said, "Behold the Lamb of God." This is the most ancient symbol used to represent the Son of God.

Triquetra

In Latin, *triquetra* means three-cornered. The symbol demonstrates the simultaneous distinction and unity of the God who is Father, Son, and Holy Spirit; three persons in one God.

Chi Rho

In Greek, chi and rho are the first two letters of Christ superimposed upon one another. The Chi Rho was one of the first Christograms (a combination of letters that form an abbreviation for the name of Jesus Christ). Another popular Christogram is IHS (a monogram of the Holy Name), derived from the Greek word IHSOUS (ΙΗΣΟΥΣ) for Jesus, or referring to *Iesus Hominum Salvator*, Jesus saviour of mankind, representing the Holy Name.

Introduction

Creeds matter. They make us who we are.

From retail outlets to political candidates to national governments, everyone vies to sow their creed into the seedbed of our hearts and minds these days. They all want us to believe what they believe, carefully crafting their creeds with the hope of gaining our affirmation.

The Declaration of Independence of the United States of America contains this creedal affirmation:

> We hold these truths to be self-evident: that all men are created equal, that they are endowed by their Creator with certain unalienable rights, that among these are Life, Liberty and the pursuit of Happiness.

At the heart of America's pledge of allegiance we find this creedal claim:

> One nation under God, indivisible, with liberty and justice for all.

Every branch of the military lives by a creed. Consider the Rifleman's Creed written by Maj. Gen. William H. Rupertus, United States Marine, following the attack on Pearl Harbor.

> This is my rifle. There are many like it, but this one is mine.

> My rifle is my best friend. It is my life. I must master it as I must master my life.

My rifle, without me, is useless. Without my rifle, I am useless. I must fire my rifle true. I must shoot straighter than my enemy who is trying to kill me. I must shoot him before he shoots me. I will . . .

My rifle and myself know that what counts in this war is not the rounds we fire, the noise of our burst, or the smoke we make. We know that it is the hits that count. We will hit . . .

My rifle is human, even as I, because it is my life. Thus, I will learn it as a brother. I will learn its weaknesses, its strength, its parts, its accessories, its sights and its barrel. I will ever guard it against the ravages of weather and damage as I will ever guard my legs, my arms, my eyes and my heart against damage. I will keep my rifle clean and ready. We will become part of each other. We will . . .

Before God, I swear this creed. My rifle and myself are the defenders of my country. We are the masters of our enemy. We are the saviors of my life.

So be it, until victory is America's and there is no enemy, but peace!

Even our children's video games revolve around creeds. Interestingly, one of the more popular games uses the word "creed" in its title. *Assassin's Creed* centers around affirmations like these:

Never kill an innocent person. Always be discreet. Never compromise the brotherhood.

In Nazi Germany, two small words pressed themselves into the creedal affirmation at the heart of the extermination of six million Jews, "Hail Hitler!"

Then there's the world of commerce and retail. Littered with phrases one might call mottos or taglines or buzzwords, they hold creedal dynamics.

"Save money. Live better. Walmart."

"Think Different." (Apple)

"You're in good hands with Allstate."

They become so familiar through their ubiquitous presence we can complete the slogans ourselves. It's proof of the way creeds shape us even when we don't realize they are shaping us.

There are creeds, and then there are *creeds*. The Bible offers a number of creedal affirmations. The creed of ancient Israel, known as the Shema, reads, "Hear O Israel, The Lord is our God. The Lord is one" (Deut. 4:6). The first creed of the Church consists of three words and comes straight from Scripture, "Jesus is Lord!" (1 Cor. 12:3; Rom. 10:9).

In the early centuries after the resurrection and ascension of Jesus, the faith of the Church began to crystallize its deepest core beliefs into creeds. The faith delivered to them from the first followers of Jesus came under attack by false teachers with heretical ideas. The leaders of the Church gathered themselves for dialogue, debate, and discernment. Stories are told that many of these leaders limped or were missing limbs as a result of the torturous persecutions they suffered at the hands of the enemies of the Church. As they sought the Holy Spirit on the nature of the true faith, clarity emerged around core affirmations. What emerged from these "councils" are what we today call the ecumenical creeds. By that we mean this is the faith proclaimed by all Christians, in all places, and at all times.

These ancient creeds, spoken by billions worldwide, hold the capacity to focus, protect, connect, unite, remind, instruct, and form us into the very people of God. In our distracted culture today, the challenge is to prevent the morph into mindless weekly recitations at church. It's so easy to casually repeat these creeds—all the while losing sight of the powerful words. John Wesley himself warned that we would one day maintain a form of faith while denying its power. For believers, these creeds offer a lifelong curriculum for faith and formation. With respect to our beliefs, the Apostles' Creed is both bottom line and battle cry.

The guide in your hands or on your screen is an effort to bring particular focus to the Apostles' Creed. In the pages ahead you will be invited to a daily practice of reading Scripture, meditating or dwelling on the text, and reflecting on the teachings of some of the Church's earliest leaders. You will be invited to ask your questions, even the seemingly unaskable ones. It has been said that the heart cannot rejoice in what the mind rejects. The Christian faith has for centuries stood thoughtfully firm amid the most formidable intellectual challenges imaginable.

It's important to also recognize that sometimes our questions mask deeper issues, providing a protection against dealing with them. For example, some will not acknowledge God as "Father," contending this name is rooted in ancient patriarchal cultures and so reflects the spirit of the age rather than a revealed theological truth. All the while, this same person grew up in a home with an abusive father. The unhealed wounds serve to keep them at bay from the healing love of the Father, as they cloak themselves in philosophical meanderings.

The seven weeks ahead offer ample opportunity to delve deep into the biblical world of this great creed seeking instruction, correction, understanding, healing, revelation, and transformation.

Give yourself to this season of exploration that you might more deeply possess your faith; be more deeply possessed by Father, Son, and Holy Spirit; and become more deeply united to fellow believers.

Near the end of his brief life, Rich Mullins put the Apostles' Creed to music. The refrain captures the essence of a study like this.

I believe, yes, I believe. It's what makes me who I am. I did not make it. No, it is making me. It is the very truth of God and not the invention of any man.

Creeds matter. They make us who we are.

Apostles' Creed

I believe in God, the Father Almighty,
creator of heaven and earth,
I believe in Jesus Christ, His only Son, our Lord,
who was conceived by the Holy Spirit,
born of the Virgin Mary,
suffered under Pontius Pilate;
was crucified, died and was buried.
He descended to the dead.
The third day He rose again from the dead.
He ascended into heaven and sits at the right hand of God the Father
Almighty. From there, He shall come to judge the living and the dead.
I believe in the Holy Spirit,
the holy catholic Church,
the communion of saints,
the forgiveness of sins, the resurrection of the body,
and the life everlasting.

CREED

Week 1

*I Believe in God, the Father Almighty,
Creator of Heaven and Earth*

Day 1: *In the Beginning*

READ

Genesis 1:1–2:2

*In the beginning God created the heavens and the earth. Now the earth was formless
and empty, darkness was over the surface of the deep, and the Spirit of God was
hovering over the waters.*

*And God said, "Let there be light," and there was light. God saw that the
light was good, and he separated the light from the darkness. God called the light
"day," and the darkness he called "night." And there was evening, and there was
morning—the first day.*

*And God said, "Let there be an expanse between the waters to separate
water from water." So God made the expanse and separated the water under
the expanse from the water above it. And it was so. God called the expanse "sky."
And there was evening, and there was morning—the second day.*

*And God said, "Let the water under the sky be gathered to one place, and let
dry ground appear." And it was so. God called the dry ground "land," and the*

gathered waters he called "seas." And God saw that it was good.

Then God said, "Let the land produce vegetation: seed-bearing plants and trees on the land that bear fruit with seed in it, according to their various kinds." And it was so. The land produced vegetation: plants bearing seed according to their kinds and trees bearing fruit with seed in it according to their kinds. And God saw that it was good. And there was evening, and there was morning—the third day.

And God said, "Let there be lights in the expanse of the sky to separate the day from the night, and let them serve as signs to mark seasons and days and years, and let them be lights in the expanse of the sky to give light on the earth." And it was so. God made two great lights—the greater light to govern the day and the lesser light to govern the night. He also made the stars. God set them in the expanse of the sky to give light on the earth, to govern the day and the night, and to separate light from darkness. And God saw that it was good. And there was evening, and there was morning—the fourth day.

And God said, "Let the water teem with living creatures, and let birds fly above the earth across the expanse of the sky." So God created the great creatures of the sea and every living and moving thing with which the water teems, according to their kinds, and every winged bird according to its kind. And God saw that it was good. God blessed them and said, "Be fruitful and increase in number and fill the water in the seas, and let the birds increase on the earth." And there was evening, and there was morning—the fifth day.

And God said, "Let the land produce living creatures according to their kinds: livestock, creatures that move along the ground, and wild animals, each according to its kind." And it was so. God made the wild animals according to their kinds, the livestock according to their kinds, and all the creatures that move along the ground according to their kinds. And God saw that it was good.

Then God said, "Let us make man in our image, in our likeness, and let them rule over the fish of the sea and the birds of the air, over the livestock, over all the earth, and over all the creatures that move along the ground."

So God created man in his own image, in the image of God he created him; male and female he created them.

God blessed them and said to them, "Be fruitful and increase in number; fill the earth and subdue it. Rule over the fish of the sea and the birds of the air and over every living creature that moves on the ground."

Then God said, "I give you every seed-bearing plant on the face of the whole earth and every tree that has fruit with seed in it. They will be yours for food. And to all the beasts of the earth and all the birds of the air and all the creatures that move on the ground—everything that has the breath of life in it—I give every green plant for food." And it was so.

God saw all that he had made, and it was very good. And there was evening, and there was morning—the sixth day.

Thus the heavens and the earth were completed in all their vast array.

By the seventh day God had finished the work he had been doing; so on the seventh day he rested from all his work. And God blessed the seventh day and made it holy, because on it he rested from all the work of creating that he had done.

MEDITATE

Underline the recurring phrases throughout this opening passage of Scripture. (hint: "And God said," "And God saw," etc.) List the phrases below.

For a moment, suspend any propensity to read Genesis 1 from a scientific method or worldview and ponder these phrases: "God said. And it was so. And God saw that it was good. And there was evening and there was morning . . ." Repeat the phrases aloud over and over so your ears can hear. Mull the words over in your mind so your eyes can see. Ponder them in your heart and behold the awesome God of such creative power, sovereign order, and unparalleled beauty.

REFLECT

I believe in God the Father. Notice how quickly it's said, and how much it's worth. He's God, and he's Father; God in power, Father in goodness. How lucky we are to have discovered that our God is our Father! So let us believe in him and promise ourselves everything from his kindness and mercy, because he is almighty. That's why we believe in God the Father almighty.

Nobody must say, "He can't forgive me my sins."

"How can't he, being almighty?"

And I say, "But he's almighty."

And you: "I've committed such sins as I can't possibly be cleansed and delivered from."

I reply, "But he's almighty."

Notice what you sing to him in the psalm: "Bless the Lord, my soul," it says, "and do not forget his recompenses, who shows himself gracious to all your iniquities, who heals all your weaknesses" (Ps. 103:2–3). That's what we need him to be almighty for.

The whole of creation needs this, of course, in order to be created; he is almighty for making heavenly things and earthly things, almighty for making immortal things and mortal things, almighty for making spiritual things and material things, almighty for making visible things and invisible things; great in the great things, and not small in the least things; in a word, he is almighty for making whatever he has wished to make.

I mean, let me tell you how many things he can't do. He can't die, he can't sin, he can't lie, he can't be deceived or mistaken; so many things he can't do, and if he could do them he wouldn't be almighty. So believe in him and confess him; For with the heart one believes unto justice, but with the mouth one makes confession unto salvation (Rom. 10:10). That's why, once you have believed, you must confess, when you give back the Symbol. So receive now what you are to retain, and afterward to give back, and never to forget.

—From a sermon on the Creed
St. Augustine of Hippo, 5th century

ASK
Express your questions, doubts, curiosities, and conundrums.

AFFIRM
Write any fresh affirmation stirring in your heart and mind from today.

Now affirm the Apostles' Creed aloud:

I believe in God, the Father Almighty, creator of heaven and earth, I believe in Jesus Christ, His only Son, our Lord . . .

Day 2: *And They Felt No Shame*

READ

Genesis 2:4–25

This is the account of the heavens and the earth when they were created.

When the Lord God made the earth and the heavens—and no shrub of the field had yet appeared on the earth and no plant of the field had yet sprung up, for the Lord God had not sent rain on the earth and there was no man to work the ground, but streams came up from the earth and watered the whole surface of the ground— the Lord God formed the man from the dust of the ground and breathed into his nostrils the breath of life, and the man became a living being.

Now the Lord God had planted a garden in the east, in Eden; and there he put the man he had formed. And the Lord God made all kinds of trees grow out of the ground—trees that were pleasing to the eye and good for food. In the middle of the garden were the tree of life and the tree of the knowledge of good and evil.

A river watering the garden flowed from Eden; from there it was separated into four headwaters. The name of the first is the Pishon; it winds through the entire land of Havilah, where there is gold. (The gold of that land is good; aromatic resin and onyx are also there.) The name of the second river is the Gihon; it winds through the entire land of Cush. The name of the third river is the Tigris; it runs along the east side of Asshur. And the fourth river is the Euphrates.

The Lord God took the man and put him in the Garden of Eden to work it and take care of it. *And the Lord God commanded the man, "You are free to eat from any tree in the garden; but you must not eat from the tree of the knowledge of good and evil, for when you eat of it you will surely die."*

The Lord God said, "It is not good for the man to be alone. *I will make a helper suitable for him."*

Now the Lord God had formed out of the ground all the beasts of the field and all the birds of the air. He brought them to the man to see what he would name them; and whatever the man called each living creature, that was its name. So the man gave names to all the livestock, the birds of the air and all the beasts of the field.

But for Adam no suitable helper was found. So the Lord God caused the man to fall into a deep sleep; and while he was sleeping, he took one of the man's ribs and closed up the place with flesh. Then the Lord God made a woman from the rib he had taken out of the man, and he brought her to the man.

The man said,

"This is now bone of my bones
and flesh of my flesh;
she shall be called 'woman,'
for she was taken out of man."

For this reason a man will leave his father and mother and be united to his wife, and they will become one flesh.

The man and his wife were both naked, and they felt no shame.

MEDITATE

As you read through the text, perhaps a verse or phrase stood out to you. Copy that phrase down here in a slow, deliberative fashion. If not, then choose one of the bolded verses from the passage and copy it in your handwriting. As a way of meditating, write the verse or phrase you selected five times, slowly, one after the other. Then rewrite the text or rephrase it in your own words (i. e., God gave the man a job: to care for the garden). As you did this exercise, did any insight or epiphany come forth? Note it here.

REFLECT

If you want to know why we call our God Father, listen to Moses: "Is he not your Father who created you, who made you and established you?" (Deut. 32:6).

Listen too to Isaiah: "O Lord, you are our Father; we are the clay, and you are the potter; we are all the work of your hand" (Isa. 64:8). Under prophetic inspiration Isaiah speaks plainly. God is our Father, not by nature, but by grace and by adoption. Paul too was a father: father of the Christians in Corinth. Not because he had begotten them according to the flesh, but because he had regenerated them according to the Spirit.

Christ when his body was fastened to the cross saw Mary, his mother according to the flesh, and John, the disciple most dear to him, and said to John: "Behold your mother," and to Mary: "Behold your son." Christ called Mary John's mother, not because she had begotten him, but because she loved him (John 19:26–27).

Joseph too was called father of Christ, not as procreator in a physical sense, but as his guardian: he was to nourish and protect him.

With greater reason God calls himself Father of human beings and wants to be called Father by us. What unspeakable generosity! He dwells in the heavens; we live on the earth. He has created the ages; we live in time. He holds the world in his hand; we are but grasshoppers on the face of the earth.

—From *God is Father*
Cyril of Jerusalem, 4th century

ASK

Express your questions, doubts, curiosities, and conundrums.

AFFIRM

Write any fresh affirmation stirring in your heart and mind from today.

Now affirm the Apostles' Creed aloud:

I believe in God, the Father Almighty, creator of heaven and earth, I believe in Jesus Christ, His only Son, our Lord . . .

Day 3: *By Him We Cry, "Abba, Father"*

READ

Romans 8:15–17

> *For you did not receive a spirit that makes you a slave again to fear, but you received the Spirit of sonship. And by him we cry, "Abba, Father." The Spirit himself testifies with our spirit that we are God's children. Now if we are children, then we are heirs— heirs of God and co-heirs with Christ, if indeed we share in his sufferings in order that we may also share in his glory.*

Galatians 4:1–7

> *What I am saying is that as long as the heir is a child, he is no different from a slave, although he owns the whole estate. He is subject to guardians and trustees until the time set by his father. So also, when we were children, we were in slavery under the basic principles of the world. But when the time had fully come, God sent his Son, born of a woman, born under law, to redeem those under law, that we might receive the full rights of sons.*
>
> *Because you are sons, God sent the Spirit of his Son into our hearts, the Spirit who calls out, "Abba, Father." So you are no longer a slave, but a son; and since you are a son, God has made you also an heir.*

MEDITATE

Invite the Holy Spirit to aid you in addressing God as "Abba, Father." Speak this most intimate name of affection a child would use for their "Daddy," over and over. Did you find this difficult? Awkward? Forced or natural? If you feel resistance to this way of addressing God, ask yourself where the resistance comes from. What makes it difficult for you to conceive of and believe in God as a good Father? So often the failure of our earthly fathers makes it very challenging to approach and believe in God as a good and loving Father. Invite the Holy Spirit to begin or deepen a process of healing in your life. Pray for the healing and restoration of your vision of God as loving Father. It will take time.

REFLECT

This relationship also involves *love*. If God be my Father, he loves me. And oh, how he loves me! When God is a Husband he is the best of husbands. Widows, somehow or other, are always well cared for. When God is a Friend, he is the best of friends, and sticketh closer than a brother; and when he is a Father he is the best of fathers. O fathers! perhaps ye do not know how much ye love your children. When they are sick ye find it out, for ye stand by their couches and ye pity them, as their little frames are writhing in pain. Well, "like as a father pitieth his children, so the Lord pitieth them that fear him." Ye know how ye love your children too, when they grieve you by their sin; anger arises, and you are ready to chasten them, but no sooner is the tear in their eye, than your hand is heavy, and you feel that you had rather smite yourself than smite them; and every time you smite them you seem to cry, "Oh that I should have thus to afflict my child for his sin! Oh that I could suffer in his stead!" And God, even our Father, "doth not afflict willingly." Is not that a sweet thing? He is, as it were, compelled to it; even the Eternal arm is not willing to do it; it is only his great love and deep wisdom that brings down the blow.

—From "The Fatherhood of God"
Charles Spurgeon

13

ASK

Express your questions, doubts, curiosities, and conundrums.

AFFIRM

Write any fresh affirmation stirring in your heart and mind from today.

Now affirm the Apostles' Creed aloud:

I believe in God, the Father Almighty, creator of heaven and earth, I believe in Jesus Christ, His only Son, our Lord . . .

Day 4: *Who Is This King of Glory?*

READ

Psalm 24

The earth is the Lord's, and everything in it,
    the world, and all who live in it;
for he founded it upon the seas
    and established it upon the waters.
Who may ascend the hill of the Lord?
    Who may stand in his holy place?
He who has clean hands and a pure heart,
    who does not lift up his soul to an idol
    or swear by what is false.
He will receive blessing from the Lord
    and vindication from God his Savior.
Such is the generation of those who seek him,
    who seek your face, O God of Jacob. Selah
Lift up your heads, O you gates;
    be lifted up, you ancient doors,
    that the King of glory may come in.
Who is this King of glory?
    The Lord strong and mighty,
    the Lord mighty in battle.
Lift up your heads, O you gates;
    lift them up, you ancient doors,
    that the King of glory may come in.
Who is he, this King of glory?
    The Lord Almighty—
    he is the King of glory. Selah

MEDITATE

"The earth is the Lord's, and everything in it, the world, and all who live in it" (Ps. 24:1). Meditate on this phrase as an affirmation of faith. Let your mind swell with the expansive content of "everything in it." Imagine now the Lord coming to his Creation, standing at the gates and preparing to enter as the King of glory. Imagine now this God knocking on the gate of your life. Declare to the gates of your heart, "Lift up your heads, O you gates . . . that the King of glory may come in" (Ps. 24:7).

Do you know the song "Clean Hands" by Charlie Hall? If not, do a quick search online and listen to the lyrics. Sing the song as an act of meditative prayer.

REFLECT

I want creation to penetrate you with so much admiration that everywhere, wherever you may be, the least plant may bring to you the clear remembrance of the Creator . . . One blade of grass or one speck of dust is enough to occupy your entire mind in beholding the art with which it has been made.

—From *The Germination of the Earth*
Basil the Great

ASK

Express your questions, doubts, curiosities, and conundrums.

AFFIRM

Write any fresh affirmation stirring in your heart and mind from today.

Now affirm the Apostles' Creed aloud:

I believe in God, the Father Almighty, creator of heaven and earth, I believe in Jesus Christ, His only Son, our Lord . . .

Day 5: *The Skies Proclaim the Work of His Hands*

READ

Psalm 19

> *The heavens declare the glory of God;*
> > *the skies proclaim the work of his hands.*
> *Day after day they pour forth speech;*
> > *night after night they display knowledge.*
> *There is no speech or language*
> > *where their voice is not heard.*
> *Their voice goes out into all the earth,*
> > *their words to the ends of the world.*
> *In the heavens he has pitched a tent for the sun,*
> > *which is like a bridegroom coming forth from his pavilion,*
> > *like a champion rejoicing to run his course.*
> *It rises at one end of the heavens*
> > *and makes its circuit to the other;*
> > *nothing is hidden from its heat.*
> *The law of the Lord is perfect,*
> > *reviving the soul.*
> *The statutes of the Lord are trustworthy,*
> > *making wise the simple.*
> *The precepts of the Lord are right,*
> > *giving joy to the heart.*
> *The commands of the Lord are radiant,*
> > *giving light to the eyes.*

The fear of the Lord is pure,
  enduring forever.
The ordinances of the Lord are sure
  and altogether righteous.
They are more precious than gold,
  than much pure gold;
they are sweeter than honey,
  than honey from the comb.
By them is your servant warned;
  in keeping them there is great reward.
Who can discern his errors?
  Forgive my hidden faults.
Keep your servant also from willful sins;
  may they not rule over me.
Then will I be blameless,
  innocent of great transgression.
May the words of my mouth and the meditation of my heart
  be pleasing in your sight,
  O Lord, my Rock and my Redeemer.

MEDITATE

Psalm 19 captures what many have called the two books of revelation: the Creation itself and the Torah (the law or Word of God). Everything God creates points back to God. Every word God speaks reveals more of his nature. Tonight, go outdoors where you might catch a glimpse of the moon and the stars. While there, recite aloud, "The heavens declare the glory of God; the skies proclaim the work of his hands." Meditate on how they speak of the glory of God through their speechlessness. In the morning, wake early enough to catch the sunrise, and behold the sun springing forth from its pavilion like a champion rejoicing to race across the sky and with every move to shout glory through its brilliant silence. Consider that a degree closer and we would burn up; a degree further away and we would freeze to death. This sun is not a god as so many in history have supposed. No, it points to the God who created it.

Learn to read the book of Creation and to receive its revelation with an ever awakening freshness. Meditate and think on these things. God has ordered our days, weeks, months, and seasons in rhythmic patterns that reveal his brilliant reality.

REFLECT

Let the truth of God sink into your soul to be its foundation stone. God is One, without beginning and without change. There was no one before him who caused him to be, and he will not have anyone after him. He has not had a beginning and he will not ever have an end. He is good and just.

God is One and he has created souls and bodies, heaven and earth.

He is the maker of everything, yet the Father of an only Son before time began: our Lord Jesus Christ through whom he has made all things visible and invisible. God the Father of our Lord Jesus Christ is not restricted to any one place: not even the heavens can contain him. On the contrary, the heavens are the work of his fingers and it is he who holds the universe in his hands. He is in everything and yet also beyond everything.

Do not imagine that the sun can shine more brightly than he or be as great as he. It was God who created the sun and therefore he is proportionately more magnificent and more brilliant.

He knows what will happen in the future. He is more powerful than anyone. He knows everything and does everything in accordance with his own will. He is not subject to the vicissitudes of time; he does not depend on others; he is not the victim of destiny. He is perfect in everything and possesses all the virtues in their fullness. He it is who has prepared a crown for the righteous.

—From *The Foundation Stone of the Soul*
Cyril of Jerusalem, 4th century

ASK

Express your questions, doubts, curiosities, and conundrums.

AFFIRM

Write any fresh affirmation stirring in your heart and mind from today.

Now affirm the Apostles' Creed aloud:

I believe in God, the Father Almighty, creator of heaven and earth, I believe in Jesus Christ, His only Son, our Lord . . .

Day 6: *Now the Serpent*

READ

Genesis 3:1–24

Now the serpent was more crafty than any of the wild animals the LORD God had made. He said to the woman, "Did God really say, 'You must not eat from any tree in the garden'?"

The woman said to the serpent, "We may eat fruit from the trees in the garden, but God did say, 'You must not eat fruit from the tree that is in the middle of the garden, and you must not touch it, or you will die.'"

"You will not surely die," the serpent said to the woman. "For God knows that when you eat of it your eyes will be opened, and you will be like God, knowing good and evil."

When the woman saw that the fruit of the tree was good for food and pleasing to the eye, and also desirable for gaining wisdom, she took some and ate it. She also gave some to her husband, who was with her, and he ate it. Then the eyes of both of them were opened, and they realized they were naked; so they sewed fig leaves together and made coverings for themselves.

Then the man and his wife heard the sound of the Lord God as he was walking in the garden in the cool of the day, and they hid from the Lord God among the trees of the garden. But the Lord God called to the man, "Where are you?"

He answered, "I heard you in the garden, and I was afraid because I was naked; so I hid."

And he said, "Who told you that you were naked? Have you eaten from the tree that I commanded you not to eat from?"

The man said, "The woman you put here with me—she gave me some fruit from the tree, and I ate it."

Then the Lord God said to the woman, "What is this you have done?"
The woman said, "The serpent deceived me, and I ate."
So the Lord God said to the serpent, "Because you have done this,
"Cursed are you above all the livestock
　and all the wild animals!
You will crawl on your belly
　and you will eat dust
　all the days of your life.
And I will put enmity
　between you and the woman,
　and between your offspring and hers;
he will crush your head,
　and you will strike his heel."
To the woman he said,
"I will greatly increase your pains in childbearing;
　with pain you will give birth to children.
Your desire will be for your husband,
　and he will rule over you."
To Adam he said, "Because you listened to your wife and ate from the tree
about which I commanded you, 'You must not eat of it,'
　"Cursed is the ground because of you;
　　through painful toil you will eat of it
　　all the days of your life.
　It will produce thorns and thistles for you,
　　and you will eat the plants of the field.
　By the sweat of your brow
　　you will eat your food
　until you return to the ground,
　　since from it you were taken;

> *for dust you are*
> *and to dust you will return."*
> Adam named his wife Eve, because she would become the mother of all the living.
> *The Lord God made garments of skin for Adam and his wife and clothed them.*
> *And the Lord God said, "The man has now become like one of us, knowing good*
> *and evil. He must not be allowed to reach out his hand and take also from the tree*
> *of life and eat, and live forever." So the Lord God banished him from the Garden*
> *of Eden to work the ground from which he had been taken. After he drove the man*
> *out, he placed on the east side of the Garden of Eden cherubim and a flaming sword*
> *flashing back and forth to guard the way to the tree of life.*

MEDITATE

Did any particular phrase or verse capture your attention in the reading? If so, pay attention. The Holy Spirit may be bringing this to mind for a particular reason. If not, consider the bolded text. Meditate on what it would be like to walk with the Lord God in the cool of the day through beautiful gardens. Now roll these words around in your mind, "And they hid from the Lord God." Speak these words of God aloud as though God were speaking them to you, "Where are you?" Locate your present condition of life and faith on the continuum below:

Walking with God————————————————————Hiding from God

REFLECT

I believe that God created me, along with all creatures. God gave to me: body and soul, eyes, ears and all the other parts of my body, my mind and all my senses and preserves them as well. God gives me clothing and shoes, food and drink, house and land, spouse and children, fields, animals, and all I own. Every day God abundantly provides everything I need to nourish this body and life. God protects me against all danger, shields and defends me from all evil. God does all this because of pure, fatherly, and divine goodness and mercy, not because I've earned it or deserved it. For all of this, I must thank, praise, serve, and obey God. Yes, this is true!

—From *The Small Catechism*
Martin Luther

ASK

Express your questions, doubts, curiosities, and conundrums.

AFFIRM

Write any fresh affirmation stirring in your heart and mind from today.

Now affirm the Apostles' Creed aloud:

I believe in God, the Father Almighty, creator of heaven and earth, I believe in Jesus Christ, His only Son, our Lord . . .

Week 2

I Believe in Jesus Christ,
His Only Son, Our Lord

READ

John 1:1–18

> *In the beginning was the Word, and the Word was with God, and the Word was God. He was with God in the beginning.*
>
> **Through him all things were made; without him nothing was made that has been made.** *In him was life, and that life was the light of men. The light shines in the darkness, but the darkness has not understood it.*
>
> *There came a man who was sent from God; his name was John. He came as a witness to testify concerning that light, so that through him all men might believe. He himself was not the light; he came only as a witness to the light. The true light that gives light to every man was coming into the world.*
>
> *He was in the world, and though the world was made through him, the world did not recognize him. He came to that which was his own, but his own did not receive him. Yet to all who received him, to those who believed in his name, he gave the right to*

become children of God—children born not of natural descent, nor of human decision or a husband's will, but born of God.

The Word became flesh and made his dwelling among us. We have seen his glory, the glory of the One and Only, who came from the Father, full of grace and truth.

John testifies concerning him. He cries out, saying, "This was he of whom I said, 'He who comes after me has surpassed me because he was before me.'" From the fullness of his grace we have all received one blessing after another. For the law was given through Moses; grace and truth came through Jesus Christ. No one has ever seen God, but God the One and Only, who is at the Father's side, has made him known.

MEDITATE

Did any particular phrase or verse capture your attention in the reading? If so, pay attention. The Holy Spirit may be bringing this to mind for a particular reason. If not, consider the bolded text. The Creed moves us from the Father as the almighty maker of Heaven and Earth to the Son. Ponder the revealed fact that Jesus Christ is also instrumental in Creation. "Through him all things were made." Speak this sentence aloud a few times so your ears can hear. Now add what may seem a redundant clause, "without him nothing was made that has been made." Speak this one aloud a few times. Now speak the whole sentence aloud. Now take a look around the natural environment and consider that all you see was made through Jesus Christ.

(Note: Keep in mind we are not searching for neatly defined scriptural principles to apply to our lives in these exercises. We are actually moving away from "ourselves" to become immersed in the expansive and glorious reality of our God. While these exercises may not feel so "practical" to your day, sustaining this kind of meditation on the Godhead will lead to something infinitely more practical.)

REFLECT

The Son, who is the Word of the Father, the very and eternal God, of one substance with the Father, took man's nature in the womb of the blessed Virgin; so that two whole and perfect natures, that is to say, the Godhead and Manhood, were joined together in one person, never to be divided; whereof is one Christ, very God and very Man, who truly suffered, was crucified, dead, and buried, to reconcile his Father to us, and to be a sacrifice, not only for original guilt, but also for actual sins of men.

—From *The Articles of Religion of the Methodist Church*
"Article 2: Of the Word, or Son of God,
Who Was Made Very Man"

ASK

Express your questions, doubts, curiosities, and conundrums.

AFFIRM

Write any fresh affirmation stirring in your heart and mind from today.

Now affirm the Apostles' Creed aloud:

I believe in God, the Father Almighty, creator of heaven and earth, I believe in Jesus Christ, His only Son, our Lord . . .

Day 2: *The Radiance of God's Glory*

READ

Hebrews 1:1–4

> *In the past God spoke to our forefathers through the prophets at many times and in various ways, but in these last days he has spoken to us by his Son, whom he appointed heir of all things, and through whom he made the universe.* **The Son is the radiance of God's glory and the exact representation of his being, sustaining all things by his powerful word.** *After he had provided purification for sins, he sat down at the right hand of the Majesty in heaven. So he became as much superior to the angels as the name he has inherited is superior to theirs.*

MEDITATE

Meditate on the word "radiance." How do you define it? What do you consider as "radiant"? Speak to God, saying, "Jesus, you are the radiance of God's glory." To that add, "You are the exact representation of God." So often people speak in the terms of "Jesus and God," when in fact, Jesus is God. Roll this phrase around in your mind, "When I see Jesus, I see God." Finally, speak to God saying, "Jesus, you sustain all things by the power of your word." Think about how inclusive the term "all" is. One last prayer, "Jesus, my God, you sustain me by the power of your word." Now write these prayers below in a slow and deliberative fashion.

REFLECT

Immortal, invisible, God only wise,
In light inaccessible hid from our eyes,
Most blessèd, most glorious, the Ancient of Days,
Almighty, victorious, Thy great Name we praise.

All laud we would render; O help us to see
'Tis only the splendor of light hideth Thee,
And so let Thy glory, Almighty, impart,
Through Christ in His story, Thy Christ to the heart.

—From *Hymns of Christ and the Christian Life*, 1876
Walter C. Smith

ASK

Express your questions, doubts, curiosities, and conundrums.

AFFIRM

Write any fresh affirmation stirring in your heart and mind from today.

Now affirm the Apostles' Creed aloud:

I believe in God, the Father Almighty, creator of heaven and earth, I believe in Jesus Christ, His only Son, our Lord . . .

Day 3: *For God Was Pleased*

READ

Colossians 1:15–23

> *He is the image of the invisible God, the firstborn over all creation. For by him all things were created: things in heaven and on earth, visible and invisible, whether thrones or powers or rulers or authorities; all things were created by him and for him. He is before all things, and in him all things hold together. And he is the head of the body, the church; he is the beginning and the firstborn from among the dead, so that in everything he might have the supremacy. For God was pleased to have all his fullness dwell in him, and through him to reconcile to himself all things, whether things on earth or things in heaven, by making peace through his blood, shed on the cross.*
>
> *Once you were alienated from God and were enemies in your minds because of your evil behavior. But now he has reconciled you by Christ's physical body through death to present you holy in his sight, without blemish and free from accusation—if you continue in your faith, established and firm, not moved from the hope held out in the gospel. This is the gospel that you heard and that has been proclaimed to every creature under heaven, and of which I, Paul, have become a servant.*

MEDITATE

Get in your mind's eye one of your closest friends. Picture them. Now ponder this question, "What if (friend's name) were the God of the cosmos?" It can be all too easy to pass over a sentence like, "For God was pleased to have all his fullness dwell in him," and hardly consider it. The implications are mind-blowing. God, the uncreated Creator of all that is, exists in fullness, in completeness in a single human being. Said another way, a single human being, Jesus Christ, exactly the same as the friend you named above, except without sin, is God. How might we be shaken from our religious familiarity into an awakening of this unfathomable truth?

REFLECT

I cannot understand how these people, who pillage this wonderful and noble economy of the Only Begotten, connect a man to him in terms of a relationship adorned with external honours and radiant in a glory which is not his, for then he is not truly God but someone who has fellowship and participation with God, and is thus a falsely-named son, a saved saviour, a redeemed redeemer.

—From *On the Unity of Christ*
Cyril of Alexandria

ASK

Express your questions, doubts, curiosities, and conundrums.

AFFIRM

Write any fresh affirmation stirring in your heart and mind from today.

Now affirm the Apostles' Creed aloud:

I believe in God, the Father Almighty, creator of heaven and earth, I believe in Jesus Christ, His only Son, our Lord . . .

Day 4: *That You May Know Him Better*

READ

Ephesians 1:15–23

> *For this reason, ever since I heard about your faith in the Lord Jesus and your love for all the saints, I have not stopped giving thanks for you, remembering you in my prayers.* **I keep asking that the God of our Lord Jesus Christ, the glorious Father, may give you the Spirit of wisdom and revelation, so that you may know him better.** *I pray also that the eyes of your heart may be enlightened in order that you may know the hope to which he has called you, the riches of his glorious inheritance in the saints, and his incomparably great power for us who believe. That power is like the working of his mighty strength, which he exerted in Christ when he raised him from the dead and seated him at his right hand in the heavenly realms, far above all rule and authority, power and dominion, and every title that can be given, not only in the present age but also in the one to come. And God placed all things under his feet and appointed him to be head over everything for the church, which is his body, the fullness of him who fills everything in every way.*

MEDITATE

Dwell on this thought: This God, our Father, who created all that is and who took on flesh in the person of Jesus Christ, wants us to know him better. Take the bolded phrase above and form it into your own prayer, "Father, please give me the Spirit of wisdom and revelation so that I may know you better and your Son, Jesus Christ." Consider that we cannot know God better without God's help. It is not purely a matter of our choice, but a combination of our willingness and his help. Prayerfully open yourself up to "the Spirit of wisdom and revelation." Actively welcome the Spirit of wisdom and revelation into your inmost being.

REFLECT

When Jesus came into the region of Caesarea Philippi, He asked His disciples, saying, "Who do men say that I, the Son of Man, am?" So they said, "Some say John the Baptist, some Elijah, and others Jeremiah or one of the prophets." He said to them, "But who do you say that I am?" Simon Peter answered and said, "You are the Christ, the Son of the living God." Jesus answered and said to him, "Blessed are you, Simon Bar-Jonah, for flesh and blood has not revealed this to you, but My Father who is in heaven."

—Matthew 16:13–17

ASK

Express your questions, doubts, curiosities, and conundrums.

AFFIRM

Write any fresh affirmation stirring in your heart and mind from today.

Now affirm the Apostles' Creed aloud:

I believe in God, the Father Almighty, creator of heaven and earth, I believe in Jesus Christ, His only Son, our Lord . . .

Day 5: *I Am*

READ

John 6:35

Then Jesus declared, "I am the bread of life. He who comes to me will never go hungry, and he who believes in me will never be thirsty."

John 8:12

When Jesus spoke again to the people, he said, "I am the light of the world. Whoever follows me will never walk in darkness, but will have the light of life."

John 10:7–10

Therefore Jesus said again, "I tell you the truth, I am the gate for the sheep. All who ever came before me were thieves and robbers, but the sheep did not listen to them. I am the gate; whoever enters through me will be saved. He will come in and go out, and find pasture. The thief comes only to steal and kill and destroy; I have come that they may have life, and have it to the full."

John 10:14

"I am the good shepherd; I know my sheep and my sheep know me—just as the Father knows me and I know the Father—and I lay down my life for the sheep."

John 11:25–26

Jesus said to her, "I am the resurrection and the life. He who believes in me will live, even though he dies; and whoever lives and believes in me will never die. Do you believe this?"

John 14:6–7

Jesus answered, "I am the way and the truth and the life. No one comes to the Father except through me. If you really knew me, you would know my Father as well. From now on, you do know him and have seen him."

John 15:1–5

"I am the true vine, and my Father is the gardener. He cuts off every branch in me that bears no fruit, while every branch that does bear fruit he prunes so that it will be even more fruitful. You are already clean because of the word I have spoken to you. Remain in me, and I will remain in you. No branch can bear fruit by itself; it must remain in the vine. Neither can you bear fruit unless you remain in me.

"I am the vine; you are the branches. If a man remains in me and I in him, he will bear much fruit; apart from me you can do nothing."

MEDITATE

"I believe in Jesus Christ, his only Son, our Lord." Dwell on the phrase, "our Lord." It is critical that though we say "our Lord," we also mean "my Lord." Meditate through this litany. In each line speak aloud as though reading Jesus' part, "I am the bread of life." Then respond saying, "You are my Lord."

Jesus:	I am the bread of life
Me:	You are my Lord.
Jesus:	I am the Light of the World.
Me:	You are my Lord.
Jesus:	I am the gate for the sheep.
Me:	You are my Lord.
Jesus:	I am the Good Shepherd.
Me:	You are my Lord.

Jesus:	I am the resurrection and the life.
Me:	You are my Lord.
Jesus:	I am the way and the truth and the life.
Me:	You are my Lord.
Jesus:	I am the True Vine.
Me:	You are my Lord.

REFLECT

What was in the beginning? "The Word," he says. . . . Why the Word? So that we might know that he proceeded from the mind. Why the Word? Because he was begotten without passion. Why the Word? Because he is image of the Father who begets him, showing forth the Father fully, in no way separated from him, and subsisting perfectly in himself, just as our word entirely befits our thought.

—From *Eulogies and Sermons*
Basil the Great

ASK

Express your questions, doubts, curiosities, and conundrums.

AFFIRM

Write any fresh affirmation stirring in your heart and mind from today.

Now affirm the Apostles' Creed aloud:

I believe in God, the Father Almighty, creator of heaven and earth, I believe in Jesus Christ, His only Son, our Lord . . .

Day 6: *Whoever Believes*

READ

John 3:16–21

> *For God so loved the world that he gave his one and only Son, that whoever believes in him shall not perish but have eternal life. For God did not send his Son into the world to condemn the world, but to save the world through him. Whoever believes in him is not condemned, but whoever does not believe stands condemned already because he has not believed in the name of God's one and only Son. This is the verdict: Light has come into the world, but men loved darkness instead of light because their deeds were evil. Everyone who does evil hates the light, and will not come into the light for fear that his deeds will be exposed. But whoever lives by the truth comes into the light, so that it may be seen plainly that what he has done has been done through God.*

MEDITATE

Today let us focus on this core word in the creed, "believe." Do you believe in Jesus Christ, his only Son, our Lord? Write out the celebrated verse of John 3:16 on the page below. In place of "the world" put a blank line. Now insert your name in the blank and read the passage aloud three times. Do you believe it? Place an x mark on the continuum below representing where you find yourself.

I do not believe————————————————————————————————I believe

REFLECT

It is not enough then to have some vague knowledge of Christ, or to engage in airy speculations, as they say, and to be able to talk a lot about him, but he must have his seat in our hearts within, so that we are unfeignedly joined to him, and with true affection.

—From *Notes on Ephesians*
John Calvin

ASK

Express your questions, doubts, curiosities, and conundrums.

AFFIRM

Write any fresh affirmation stirring in your heart and mind from today.

Now affirm the Apostles' Creed aloud:

I believe in God, the Father Almighty, creator of heaven and earth, I believe in Jesus Christ, His only Son, our Lord . . .

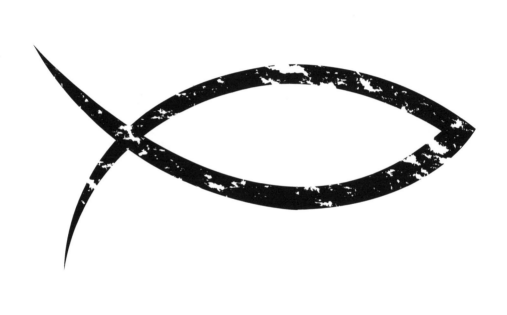

Week 3

*Who Was Conceived by the Holy Spirit, Born of
the Virgin Mary, Suffered under Pontius Pilate;
Was Crucified, Died and Was Buried*

Day 1: *In the Sixth Month*

READ

Luke 1:26–38

*In the sixth month, God sent the angel Gabriel to Nazareth, a town in Galilee, to a
virgin pledged to be married to a man named Joseph, a descendant of David. The
virgin's name was Mary. The angel went to her and said, "Greetings, you who are
highly favored! The Lord is with you."*

*Mary was greatly troubled at his words and wondered what kind of greeting this
might be. But the angel said to her, "Do not be afraid, Mary, you have found favor
with God. You will be with child and give birth to a son, and you are to give him the
name Jesus. He will be great and will be called the Son of the Most High. The Lord
God will give him the throne of his father David, and he will reign over the house of
Jacob forever; his kingdom will never end."*

"How will this be," Mary asked the angel, "since I am a virgin?"

The angel answered, "The Holy Spirit will come upon you, and the power of the Most High will overshadow you. So the holy one to be born will be called the Son of God. Even Elizabeth your relative is going to have a child in her old age, and she who was said to be barren is in her sixth month. For nothing is impossible with God."

"I am the Lord's servant," Mary answered. "May it be to me as you have said." Then the angel left her.

MEDITATE

God reveals to us through the Virgin Mary a picture of what true belief looks like. In the face of an unexpected visitor with an unbelievable claim to an unlikely person, Mary unflinchingly pledges faith-filled obedience. Take a few minutes and commit her response to memory, "I am the Lord's servant. May it be to me as you have said." This is the disciple's prayer. Invite the Holy Spirit to etch this prayer on your heart, to make it a part of your praying vocabulary.

REFLECT

The nativity mystery, "conceived from the Holy Spirit and born from the Virgin Mary," means that God became human, truly human out of his own grace. The miracle of the existence of Jesus, his "climbing down of God" is: Holy Spirit and Virgin Mary! Here is a human being, the Virgin Mary, and as he comes from God, Jesus comes also from this human being. Born of the Virgin Mary means a human origin for God. Jesus Christ is not only truly God, he is human like every one of us. He is human without limitation. He is not only similar to us, he is like us.

—From *Dogmatics in Outline*
Karl Barth

ASK

Express your questions, doubts, curiosities, and conundrums.

AFFIRM

Write any fresh affirmation stirring in your heart and mind from today.

Now affirm the Apostles' Creed aloud:

I believe in God, the Father Almighty, creator of heaven and earth, I believe in Jesus Christ, His only Son, our Lord . . .

Day 2: *Caesar Augustus Issued a Decree*

READ

Luke 2:1–20

In those days Caesar Augustus issued a decree that a census should be taken of the entire Roman world. (This was the first census that took place while Quirinius was governor of Syria.) And everyone went to his own town to register.

So Joseph also went up from the town of Nazareth in Galilee to Judea, to Bethlehem the town of David, because he belonged to the house and line of David. He went there to register with Mary, who was pledged to be married to him and was expecting a child. While they were there, the time came for the baby to be born, and she gave birth to her firstborn, a son. She wrapped him in cloths and placed him in a manger, because there was no room for them in the inn.

And there were shepherds living out in the fields nearby, keeping watch over their flocks at night. An angel of the Lord appeared to them, and the glory of the Lord shone around them, and they were terrified. But the angel said to them, "Do not be afraid. I bring you good news of great joy that will be for all the people. Today in the town of David a Savior has been born to you; he is Christ the Lord. This will be a sign to you: You will find a baby wrapped in cloths and lying in a manger."

Suddenly a great company of the heavenly host appeared with the angel, praising God and saying,

"Glory to God in the highest, and on earth peace to men on whom his favor rests."

When the angels had left them and gone into heaven, the shepherds said to one another, "Let's go to Bethlehem and see this thing that has happened, which the Lord has told us about."

So they hurried off and found Mary and Joseph, and the baby, who was lying in the manger. When they had seen him, they spread the word concerning what had been told them about this child, and all who heard it were amazed at what the shepherds said to them. But Mary treasured up all these things and pondered them in her heart. The shepherds returned, glorifying and praising God for all the things they had heard and seen, which were just as they had been told.

MEDITATE

The birth of Jesus is a fact of history. The claim that he was born of a virgin is an affirmation of faith. Though some contest even his existence, many vehemently deny the virgin birth. Birth is normal. Birth to a virgin is impossible. Just because an occurrence is categorized as an article of faith does not somehow remove it from the category of history. An article of faith takes us beyond the stage of history and into the backstage world of the Director of the drama. From this vantage point, we can see how the impossible becomes reality.

How could God really have a son? Ahhhh, conceived not by a man but by the Holy Spirit who impregnates a woman while preserving her virginity. Though it cannot be proved, it can be trusted. The Creed is not anchored in history. It is anchored in eternity, albeit through real historical events. When eternity breaks forth into history we enter the realm of faith, a place where the natural and the supernatural fuse into a new normal, where we find the very Son of God laid in a feeding trough, where the veil of the sky can be pulled back on occasion to reveal the army of angels who were always there. The Creed aims to usher us into this new normal, the place we were intended to live all along, the world where "nothing is impossible with God."

Do a little fact-checking on that phrase. See Genesis 18:10–14, Jeremiah 32:17, Luke 1:37, and Mark 14:32–36.

Now think on these things.

REFLECT

When the angel Gabriel told Mary, "You will be with child and give birth to a son," she had a simple question about the natural: How can this be since I am a virgin?! The answer had to do not with the natural but . . . something, in fact, entirely supernatural: "The Holy Spirit will come upon you, and the Most High will overshadow you" (Luke 1:35 NIV). That was too wonderful, and Mary was silent. She had no question about the supernatural. She was satisfied with God's answer. The truth about the Incarnation is a thing too wonderful for us. . . . Mary's acceptance of the angel's answer to her innocent question was immediate, though she could not imagine the intricacies and mysteries of its working in her young virgin body. She surrendered herself utterly to God in trust and obedience.

—From *Keep a Quiet Heart*
Elisabeth Elliot

ASK

Express your questions, doubts, curiosities, and conundrums.

AFFIRM

Write any fresh affirmation stirring in your heart and mind from today.

Now affirm the Apostles' Creed aloud:

I believe in God, the Father Almighty, creator of heaven and earth, I believe in Jesus Christ, His only Son, our Lord . . .

Day 3: *What Shall I Do, Then, with Jesus?*

READ

Matthew 27:22–26

> *"What shall I do, then, with Jesus who is called Christ?" Pilate asked.*
>> *They all answered, "Crucify him!"*
> *"Why? What crime has he committed?" asked Pilate.*
> *But they shouted all the louder, "Crucify him!"*
> *When Pilate saw that he was getting nowhere, but that instead an uproar was starting, he took water and washed his hands in front of the crowd.* **"I am innocent of this man's blood," he said. "It is your responsibility!"**
>> *All the people answered, "Let his blood be on us and on our children!"*
>> *Then he released Barabbas to them. But he had Jesus flogged, and handed him over to be crucified.*

MEDITATE

The Creed affirms, Jesus Christ "suffered under Pontius Pilate." But didn't Pilate try to do the right thing in releasing Jesus, in whom he found no fault? He even tried to wash his hands of guilt, blaming it on the people. Yet Pilate is forever enshrined as a villain. Of the three human beings named in the Creed, Pontius Pilate is the designated bad guy. (Though it's about twenty clicks beyond ironic, another Roman, one of Pilate's henchmen, makes the creedal claim at the cross of Jesus, "Truly this man was the son of God.")

Why do you think Pilate gets all the credit in the creed? What are the implications of this? Ponder this: Though Jesus suffered under Pontius Pilate, it was our sin that brought about his suffering.

REFLECT

It was by surrendering to death the body which He had taken, as an offering and sacrifice free from every stain, that He forthwith abolished death for His human brethren by the offering of the equivalent. For naturally, since the Word of God was above all, when He offered His own temple and bodily instrument as a substitute for the life of all, He fulfilled in death all that was required.

—From *On the Incarnation*
Athanasius

ASK

Express your questions, doubts, curiosities, and conundrums.

AFFIRM

Write any fresh affirmation stirring in your heart and mind from today.

Now affirm the Apostles' Creed aloud:

I believe in God, the Father Almighty, creator of heaven and earth, I believe in Jesus Christ, His only Son, our Lord . . .

Day 4: *And Darkness Came Over the Whole Land*

READ

Luke 23:32–46

Two other men, both criminals, were also led out with him to be executed. When they came to the place called the Skull, there they crucified him, along with the criminals— one on his right, the other on his left. Jesus said, "Father, forgive them, for they do not know what they are doing." And they divided up his clothes by casting lots.

The people stood watching, and the rulers even sneered at him. They said, "He saved others; let him save himself if he is the Christ of God, the Chosen One."

The soldiers also came up and mocked him. They offered him wine vinegar and said, "If you are the king of the Jews, save yourself."

There was a written notice above him, which read: THIS IS THE KING OF THE JEWS.

One of the criminals who hung there hurled insults at him: "Aren't you the Christ? Save yourself and us!"

But the other criminal rebuked him. "Don't you fear God," he said, "since you are under the same sentence? We are punished justly, for we are getting what our deeds deserve. But this man has done nothing wrong."

Then he said, "Jesus, remember me when you come into your kingdom."

Jesus answered him, "I tell you the truth, today you will be with me in paradise."

It was now about the sixth hour, and darkness came over the whole land until the ninth hour, for the sun stopped shining. And the curtain of the temple was torn in two. Jesus called out with a loud voice, "Father, into your hands I commit my spirit." When he had said this, he breathed his last.

MEDITATE

Note both the earthly elements of this scene of crucifixion as well as the cosmic dimensions. Criminals, rulers, soldiers, and "the people" gathered amid taunts, sneers, insults, and gambling. Meanwhile a massive story unfolds in the sanctuary of the skies and in the most holy place of the temple. It is as though the book of Creation and the book of the Covenant convulse in a cosmic conflict. At this sight, at high noon, the God who said, "Let there be light," allows the land to be shrouded in thick darkness. Simultaneously, the thick dark curtain in the temple separating the people from the "Most Holy Place," the throne room of God on Earth, rips from top to bottom. As darkness gloats over the land, the glorious presence of God slips undetected into the world to rob the darkness of its victory.

In the midst of it all, the Word made flesh keeps speaking Life. Note how his words form both prayer and answers to prayer. To a thief's prayer he responds with a promise of paradise. He responds to his tormenters by praying for their forgiveness. With his last words he affirms faith in the reality which long preceded the planet, the union of Father, Son, and Holy Spirit. In these moments, history may record an eclipse and an earthquake. The creed affirms the central event in all of time and eternity.

As an affirmation of faith, try praying these prayers of Jesus from the cross. In the first prayer, insert the word "us" and "me" for Father forgive "them." Dwell in this prayer until it comes from a place of honesty. Now turn to the prayer, "Father (Abba), into your hands I commit my spirit."

REFLECT

God allows himself to be humiliated and crucified in the Son, in order to free the oppressors and the oppressed from oppression and to open up to them the situation of free, sympathetic humanity.

—From *The Crucified God*
Jürgen Moltmann

ASK

Express your questions, doubts, curiosities, and conundrums.

AFFIRM

Write any fresh affirmation stirring in your heart and mind from today.

Now affirm the Apostles' Creed aloud:

I believe in God, the Father Almighty, creator of heaven and earth, I believe in Jesus Christ, His only Son, our Lord . . .

Day 5: *There Came a Rich Man from Arimathea*

READ

Matthew 27:57–66

> *As evening approached, there came a rich man from Arimathea, named Joseph, who had himself become a disciple of Jesus. Going to Pilate, he asked for Jesus' body, and Pilate ordered that it be given to him. Joseph took the body, wrapped it in a clean linen cloth, and placed it in his own new tomb that he had cut out of the rock. He rolled a big stone in front of the entrance to the tomb and went away. Mary Magdalene and the other Mary were sitting there opposite the tomb.*
>
> *The next day, the one after Preparation Day, the chief priests and the Pharisees went to Pilate. "Sir," they said, "we remember that while he was still alive that deceiver said, 'After three days I will rise again.' So give the order for the tomb to be made secure until the third day. Otherwise, his disciples may come and steal the body and tell the people that he has been raised from the dead. This last deception will be worse than the first."*
>
> *"Take a guard," Pilate answered. "Go, make the tomb as secure as you know how." So they went and made the tomb secure by putting a seal on the stone and posting the guard.*

MEDITATE

And so we affirm the death and burial of the Son of God. The man born to poverty whose last possession was stolen from him and gambled away is laid in a rich man's tomb. This man of wealth makes an appearance before the governor of the land in order to spend his relational capital on behalf of a dead Messiah. Joseph of Arimathea, this disciple in hiding, makes his public profession of faith in a most undignified, public fashion. He provides the tomb, lays the body inside, and seals it with a stone. And if that weren't enough, Pilate has it sealed and posts guards.

Ponder the set of this scene. The plot has arrived at the ultimate impasse of impossibility. In your mind's eye, visualize the tomb, the stone, the seal, the guards, the weapons, and the setting sun ushering in the rest of Sabbath. Fix this scene in your memory.

REFLECT

The Messiah is the ultimate interpreter of God to the world and the world to God, of God to ourselves and ourselves to God, indeed of ourselves to ourselves, assuring us that while we may have meant it for evil, God meant it for good. It is in him that we are rooted and grounded, that we find our ultimate terroir, the soil that nourishes us and makes us what we are. And, particularly, it is in him that the dark theme of suffering comes to full expression.

—From "Christ the Power of God and the Wisdom of God"
N. T. Wright

ASK

Express your questions, doubts, curiosities, and conundrums.

AFFIRM

Write any fresh affirmation stirring in your heart and mind from today.

Now affirm the Apostles' Creed aloud:

> *I believe in God, the Father Almighty, creator of heaven and earth, I believe in Jesus Christ, His only Son, our Lord . . .*

Day 6: *By This Gospel You Are Saved*

READ

1 Corinthians 15:1–8

> *Now, brothers, I want to remind you of the gospel I preached to you, which you received and on which you have taken your stand.* **By this gospel you are saved,** *if you hold firmly to the word I preached to you. Otherwise, you have believed in vain.*
>
> **For what I received I passed on to you as of first importance: that Christ died for our sins according to the Scriptures, that he was buried, that he was raised on the third day according to the Scriptures, and that he appeared to Peter, and then to the Twelve.** *After that, he appeared to more than five hundred of the brothers at the same time, most of whom are still living, though some have fallen asleep. Then he appeared to James, then to all the apostles, and last of all he appeared to me also, as to one abnormally born.*

MEDITATE

We will give focus to the resurrection in next week's readings. For now, let us gain a wider perspective or perhaps a more elevated vantage point. There is a single word to capture all of these events and happenings: *gospel*. In our parlance, the word "gospel" has come to be known as both good news and as the established truth. In this text, Paul pens the creed before the creeds. In an economy of speech he captures the gospel in such a way that it can be unleashed in the world. And isn't that what creeds do? Creeds capture the truth in ways that don't hold truth captive but rather sets it free to captivate the world.

Take a few minutes and write in your own handwriting the creedal affirmation bolded in the previous text. Read it aloud several times so your ears can hear it. Begin praying about how this gospel that has been handed down to you might be handed down through you to others. This is where affirmation of faith becomes application of faith.

REFLECT

The earthly form of Christ is the form that died on the cross. The image of God is the image of Christ crucified. It is to this image that the life of the disciples must be conformed; in other words, they must be conformed to his death (Phil. 3:10, Rom. 6:4) The Christian life is a life of crucifixion (Gal. 2:19) In baptism the form of Christ's death is impressed upon his own. They are dead to the flesh and to sin, they are dead to the world, and the world is dead to them (Gal. 6:14). Anybody living in the strength of Christ's baptism lives in the strength of Christ's death.

—From *The Cost of Discipleship*
Dietrich Bonhoeffer

ASK

Express your questions, doubts, curiosities, and conundrums.

AFFIRM

Write any fresh affirmation stirring in your heart and mind from today.

Now affirm the Apostles' Creed aloud:

I believe in God, the Father Almighty, creator of heaven and earth, I believe in Jesus Christ, His only Son, our Lord . . .

Week 4

He Descended to the Dead. The Third Day He Arose from the Dead. He Ascended into Heaven and Sits at the Right Hand of God the Father Almighty. From There, He Shall Come to Judge the Living and the Dead

Day 1: *He Went and Preached to the Spirits in Prison*

READ

1 Peter 3:18–22

> *For Christ died for sins once for all, the righteous for the unrighteous, to bring you to God. He was put to death in the body but made alive by the Spirit, through whom also he went and preached to the spirits in prison who disobeyed long ago when God waited patiently in the days of Noah while the ark was being built. In it only a few people, eight in all, were saved through water, and this water symbolizes baptism that now saves you also—not the removal of dirt from the body but the pledge of a good conscience toward God. It saves you by the resurrection of Jesus Christ, who has gone into heaven and is at God's right hand—with angels, authorities and powers in submission to him.*

MEDITATE

The redeeming work of Jesus Christ on the cross extends not only after his death but even before his life. Jesus was not taking a break on the Sabbath, what we today call "Holy Saturday." He was preaching the gospel to those whose death preceded his own so they, too, would have an opportunity to respond to the gospel. The grace of God in Christ is truly awe inspiring, covering all of time and eternity. In attempting to reach this unreachable reality, the apostle Paul wrote down his prayer for us:

"For this reason I kneel before the Father, from whom his whole family in heaven and on earth derives its name. I pray that out of his glorious riches he may strengthen you with power through his Spirit in your inner being, so that Christ may dwell in your hearts through faith. And I pray that you, being rooted and established in love, may have power, together with all the saints, to grasp how wide and long and high and deep is the love of Christ, and to know this love that surpasses knowledge—that you may be filled to the measure of all the fullness of God" (Eph. 3:14–18).

Sit with this prayer. Pray it slowly and deliberately and aloud. Kneel on the floor if possible.

REFLECT

He descended into Hades and took Hades captive! He embittered it when it tasted His flesh! And anticipating this, Isaiah exclaimed: "Hades was embittered when it encountered Thee in the lower regions."

It was embittered, for it was abolished! It was embittered, for it was mocked! It was embittered, for it was purged!

It was embittered, for it was despoiled! It was embittered, for it was bound in chains!

—From *Paschal Homily*
John Chrysostom

ASK

Express your questions, doubts, curiosities, and conundrums.

AFFIRM

Write any fresh affirmation stirring in your heart and mind from today.

Now affirm the Apostles' Creed aloud:

I believe in God, the Father Almighty, creator of heaven and earth, I believe in Jesus Christ, His only Son, our Lord . . .

Day 2: *He Is Not Here—He Is Risen*

READ

Matthew 28:1–10

> *After the Sabbath, at dawn on the first day of the week, Mary Magdalene and the other Mary went to look at the tomb.*
>
> *There was a violent earthquake, for an angel of the Lord came down from heaven and, going to the tomb, rolled back the stone and sat on it. His appearance was like lightning, and his clothes were white as snow. The guards were so afraid of him that they shook and became like dead men.*
>
> *The angel said to the women, "Do not be afraid, for I know that you are looking for Jesus, who was crucified. He is not here; he has risen, just as he said. Come and see the place where he lay. Then go quickly and tell his disciples: 'He has risen from the dead and is going ahead of you into Galilee. There you will see him.' Now I have told you."*
>
> *So the women hurried away from the tomb, afraid yet filled with joy, and ran to tell his disciples. Suddenly Jesus met them. "Greetings," he said. They came to him, clasped his feet and worshiped him. Then Jesus said to them, "Do not be afraid. Go and tell my brothers to go to Galilee; there they will see me."*

MEDITATE

The resurrection is a miracle, the magnitude of which inspires both fear and joy at the same time. Resurrection is not resuscitation. It is the very reversal of death, the ultimate and final enemy of God. Picture this unfolding in your mind's eye. The guards lying on the ground as though dead; the angelic being sitting atop the now rolled away stone; the women running to find the disciples to share this news; Jesus intercepting them on the road. Can you imagine? They fall to the ground and worship him, holding onto his feet. What a scene!

Are you there yet? Can you picture yourself at the feet of Jesus, grasping his feet? Reflect on what that would be like. What an affirmation of faith this would be.

REFLECT

The third day has returned; arise, my buried One; it is not becoming that Your limbs should lie in the lowly sepulchre, nor that worthless stones should press that which is the ransom of the world. It is unworthy that a stone should shut in with a confining rock, and cover Him in whose fist all things are enclosed. Take away the linen clothes, I pray; leave the napkins in the tomb: You are sufficient for us, and without You there is nothing. Release the chained shades of the infernal prison, and recall to the upper regions whatever sinks to the lowest depths. Give back Your face, that the world may see the light; give back the day which flees from us at Your death. But returning, O holy conqueror! You altogether filled the heaven!

—From *On Easter*
Venantius

ASK

Express your questions, doubts, curiosities, and conundrums.

AFFIRM

Write any fresh affirmation stirring in your heart and mind from today.

Now affirm the Apostles' Creed aloud:

I believe in God, the Father Almighty, creator of heaven and earth, I believe in Jesus Christ, His only Son, our Lord . . .

Day 3: *He Was Taken Up*

READ

Acts 1:6–11

> *So when they met together, they asked him, "Lord, are you at this time going to restore the kingdom to Israel?"*
>
> *He said to them: "It is not for you to know the times or dates the Father has set by his own authority. But you will receive power when the Holy Spirit comes on you; and you will be my witnesses in Jerusalem, and in all Judea and Samaria, and to the ends of the earth."*
>
> **After he said this, he was taken up before their very eyes, and a cloud hid him from their sight.**
>
> *They were looking intently up into the sky as he was going, when suddenly two men dressed in white stood beside them. "Men of Galilee," they said, "why do you stand here looking into the sky? This same Jesus, who has been taken from you into heaven, will come back in the same way you have seen him go into heaven."*

MEDITATE

He ascended into heaven. It may be the most under-celebrated and underestimated episode in the story of salvation. The One who descended all the way to the dead, now ascends all the way to heaven. Take note that Jesus did not disappear or become invisible or morph into some kind of ethereal vapor in the clouds. He ascended bodily, fully human and fully God. He did not become invisible. They simply could not see him anymore. There is a big difference. Ponder this statement: Today, seated in the heavens is a human being who rules over all that is. This is our affirmation of faith.

REFLECT

Today our Lord Jesus Christ ascended into heaven; let our hearts ascend with him. Listen to the words of the Apostle: If you have risen with Christ, set your hearts on the things that are above where Christ is, seated at the right hand of God; seek the things that are above, not the things that are on earth. For just as he remained with us even after his ascension, so we too are already in heaven with him, even though what is promised us has not yet been fulfilled in our bodies.

—From *The Ascension of Christ*
St. Augustine of Hippo

ASK

Express your questions, doubts, curiosities, and conundrums.

AFFIRM

Write any fresh affirmation stirring in your heart and mind from today.

Now affirm the Apostles' Creed aloud:

I believe in God, the Father Almighty, creator of heaven and earth, I believe in Jesus Christ, His only Son, our Lord . . .

Day 4: *I See Heaven Open*

READ

Acts 7:54–60

> *When they heard this, they were furious and gnashed their teeth at him. But Stephen, full of the Holy Spirit, looked up to heaven and saw the glory of God, and Jesus standing at the right hand of God. "Look," he said, "I see heaven open and the Son of Man standing at the right hand of God."*
>
> *At this they covered their ears and, yelling at the top of their voices, they all rushed at him, dragged him out of the city and began to stone him. Meanwhile, the witnesses laid their clothes at the feet of a young man named Saul.*
>
> *While they were stoning him, Stephen prayed, "Lord Jesus, receive my spirit." Then he fell on his knees and cried out, "Lord, do not hold this sin against them." When he had said this, he fell asleep.*

Hebrews 12:1–4

> *Therefore, since we are surrounded by such a great cloud of witnesses, let us throw off everything that hinders and the sin that so easily entangles, and let us run with perseverance the race marked out for us. Let us fix our eyes on Jesus, the author and perfecter of our faith, who for the joy set before him endured the cross, scorning its shame, and sat down at the right hand of the throne of God. Consider him who endured such opposition from sinful men, so that you will not grow weary and lose heart.*
>
> *In your struggle against sin, you have not yet resisted to the point of shedding your blood.*

MEDITATE

"Since, then, you have been raised with Christ, set your hearts on things above, where Christ is seated at the right hand of God" (Col. 3:1).

To be "in Christ" is to simultaneously dwell in heaven and live on earth. And isn't this the point: "On Earth as it is in Heaven." This is why we are instructed to set our hearts and minds on things above. What would that mean for you? We are exhorted to "fix our eyes on Jesus." Could this be what it means to have a pure heart, as in, "Blessed are the pure in heart, for they shall see God" (Matt. 5:8)? As we set our hearts and minds on things above and fix our eyes on Jesus, we become earthen vessels for the in-breaking of heaven on earth. Take five uninterrupted minutes and attempt to do this now. Do it every day for a week. Stretch it to ten minutes for the second week. Your capacity to focus and your ability to see will increase dramatically in the days to come.

REFLECT

All power to our great Lord
Is by the Father given;
By angel-hosts adored,
He reigns supreme in heaven:
Join all on earth, rejoice and sing;
Glory ascribe to glory's King.
High on his holy seat
He bears the righteous sway;
His foes beneath his feet
Shall sink and die away:
Join all on earth, rejoice and sing;
Glory ascribe to glory's King.

—From "God is Gone up High"
Charles Wesley

ASK

Express your questions, doubts, curiosities, and conundrums.

AFFIRM

Write any fresh affirmation stirring in your heart and mind from today.

Now affirm the Apostles' Creed aloud:

I believe in God, the Father Almighty, creator of heaven and earth, I believe in Jesus Christ, His only Son, our Lord . . .

Day 5: *He Will Appear a Second Time*

READ

Hebrews 9:24–28

For Christ did not enter a man-made sanctuary that was only a copy of the true one; he entered heaven itself, now to appear for us in God's presence. Nor did he enter heaven to offer himself again and again, the way the high priest enters the Most Holy Place every year with blood that is not his own. Then Christ would have had to suffer many times since the creation of the world. But now he has appeared once for all at the end of the ages to do away with sin by the sacrifice of himself. **Just as man is destined to die once, and after that to face judgment, so Christ was sacrificed once to take away the sins of many people; and he will appear a second time, not to bear sin, but to bring salvation to those who are waiting for him.**

1 Thessalonians 4:13–18

Brothers, we do not want you to be ignorant about those who fall asleep, or to grieve like the rest of men, who have no hope. We believe that Jesus died and rose again and so we believe that God will bring with Jesus those who have fallen asleep in him. According to the Lord's own word, we tell you that we who are still alive, who are left till the coming of the Lord, will certainly not precede those who have fallen asleep. For the Lord himself will come down from heaven, with a loud command, with the voice of the archangel and with the trumpet call of God, and the dead in Christ will rise first. After that, we who are still alive and are left will be caught up together with them in the clouds to meet the Lord in the air. And so we will be with the Lord forever. Therefore encourage each other with these words.

2 Thessalonians 1:5–10

> *All this is evidence that God's judgment is right, and as a result you will be counted worthy of the kingdom of God, for which you are suffering. God is just: He will pay back trouble to those who trouble you and give relief to you who are troubled, and to us as well. This will happen when the Lord Jesus is revealed from heaven in blazing fire with his powerful angels. He will punish those who do not know God and do not obey the gospel of our Lord Jesus. They will be punished with everlasting destruction and shut out from the presence of the Lord and from the majesty of his power on the day he comes to be glorified in his holy people and to be marveled at among all those who have believed. This includes you, because you believed our testimony to you.*

MEDITATE

Do you believe in the second coming of Christ and the final judgment of the human race? Are you prepared for such a time? What if he returned today? What would you do if you knew he were returning tomorrow?

REFLECT

And then shall appear the signs of the truth; first, the sign of an outspreading in heaven; then the sign of the sound of the trumpet. And third, the resurrection of the dead—yet not of all, but as it is said: "The Lord shall come and all His saints with Him". Then shall the world see the Lord coming upon the clouds of heaven.

—From *The Didache*

ASK

Express your questions, doubts, curiosities, and conundrums.

AFFIRM

Write any fresh affirmation stirring in your heart and mind from today.

Now affirm the Apostles' Creed aloud:

I believe in God, the Father Almighty, creator of heaven and earth, I believe in Jesus Christ, His only Son, our Lord . . .

Day 6: *Jesus Christ Is Lord*

READ

Philippians 2:5–11

> *Your attitude should be the same as that of Christ Jesus:*
>
> *Who, being in very nature God, did not consider equality with God something to be grasped, but made himself nothing, taking the very nature of a servant, being made in human likeness. And being found in appearance as a man, he humbled himself and became obedient to death—even death on a cross! Therefore God exalted him to the highest place and gave him the name that is above every name, that at the name of Jesus every knee should bow, in heaven and on earth and under the earth, and every tongue confess that Jesus Christ is Lord, to the glory of God the Father.*

MEDITATE

\/: Jesus, in very nature God, does not grasp at equality with God.

/\: Adam, created in the image of God, grasps for equality with God (i.e., "God knows if you eat this fruit you will be like him").

\/: Jesus makes himself nothing.

/\: Adam tries to make himself something.

\/: Jesus humbles himself.

/\: Adam takes pride in himself.

\/: Jesus comes down from heaven to die on a cross.

/\: Adam's race builds a tower from the earth in an attempt to reach the heavens (see Gen. 11:4).

$\bigvee$: Jesus is given the name that is above every name.

$\bigwedge$: Adam's race attempts to "make a name for themselves."

$\bigvee$: Jesus is raised from the dead and exalted to the highest place.

$\bigwedge$: Adam's race is destined for death and falls to the lowest place.

$\bigvee$: At the name of Jesus all the nations gather and every tongue will confess that Jesus Christ is Lord.

$\bigwedge$: Adam's race is confused in their language and scatters.

$\bigvee$: Are you following Jesus in the humble way of the cross?

$\bigwedge$: Are you following Adam in the proud way of making a name for yourself?

Take a moment and plot your location on the continuum below. What steps might you take to move further to the right?

Mind of Adam————————————————————————Mind of Christ

REFLECT

He is going to land in force; we do not know when. But we can guess why He is delaying. He wants to give us the chance of joining His side freely . . . I wonder whether people who ask God to interfere openly and directly in our world quite realize what it will be like when He does. When that happens, it is the end of the world. When the author walks on the stage the play is over. God is going to invade, all right: but what is the good of saying you are on His side then? . . . Now, today, this moment, is our chance to choose the right side. God is holding back to give us that chance. It will not last for ever. We must take it or leave it.

—From *Mere Christianity*
C. S. Lewis

ASK

Express your questions, doubts, curiosities, and conundrums.

AFFIRM

Write any fresh affirmation stirring in your heart and mind from today.

Now affirm the Apostles' Creed aloud:

I believe in God, the Father Almighty, creator of heaven and earth, I believe in Jesus Christ, His only Son, our Lord . . .

Week 5

I Believe in the Holy Spirit

READ

Joel 2:28–32

> *"And afterward, I will pour out my Spirit on all people. Your sons and daughters will prophesy, your old men will dream dreams, your young men will see visions. Even on my servants, both men and women, I will pour out my Spirit in those days. I will show wonders in the heavens and on the earth, blood and fire and billows of smoke. The sun will be turned to darkness and the moon to blood before the coming of the great and dreadful day of the Lord. And everyone who calls on the name of the Lord will be saved; for on Mount Zion and in Jerusalem there will be deliverance, as the Lord has said, among the survivors whom the Lord calls."*

Ezekiel 36:25–28

> *I will sprinkle clean water on you, and you will be clean; I will cleanse you from all your impurities and from all your idols. I will give you a new heart and put a new spirit in you; I will remove from you your heart of stone and give you a heart*

of flesh. And I will put my Spirit in you and move you to follow my decrees and be careful to keep my laws. You will live in the land I gave your forefathers; you will be my people, and I will be your God.

MEDITATE

Hoping. Longing. Waiting. Generation upon generation read these words from the prophet Joel and Ezekiel with anticipation and probably frustration. To fulfill a promise like this would renew the human race, even the face of the Earth. It is little wonder this prayer, "How long, O Lord," so frequently appears throughout Scripture. At many points, Scripture seems to say something like this, "The law was given so that the Spirit might be desired, and the Spirit was given so that the law might be obeyed." Meditate on that phrase.

So often we think of the work of Jesus Christ and the promise of the Holy Spirit as the remedy for original sin when it is far more than this. The Holy Spirit will settle for nothing less than original righteousness. The realities Joel and Ezekiel and others prophesy is not a patch or a fix or a work-around. They speak of a new operating system, a total renovation, the New Creation. There's a big difference between bypass surgery and a brand new heart. Are you thinking in this framework?

Spend a few minutes today with this ancient prayer, crafted from Scripture and passed down through the ages.

REFLECT

Come Holy Spirit, fill the hearts of your faithful and kindle in them the fire of your love. Send forth your Spirit and they shall be created. And you shall renew the face of the earth.

O, God, who by the light of the Holy Spirit, did instruct the hearts of the faithful, grant that by the same Holy Spirit we may be truly wise and ever enjoy His consolations, through Christ our Lord, Amen.

—From *Prayer to the Holy Spirit*

ASK

Express your questions, doubts, curiosities, and conundrums.

AFFIRM

Write any fresh affirmation stirring in your heart and mind from today.

Now affirm the Apostles' Creed aloud:

I believe in God, the Father Almighty, creator of heaven and earth, I believe in Jesus Christ, His only Son, our Lord . . .

Day 2: *What Does This Mean?*

READ

Acts 2:1–12

When the day of Pentecost came, they were all together in one place. Suddenly a sound like the blowing of a violent wind came from heaven and filled the whole house where they were sitting. They saw what seemed to be tongues of fire that separated and came to rest on each of them. All of them were filled with the Holy Spirit and began to speak in other tongues as the Spirit enabled them.

Now there were staying in Jerusalem God-fearing Jews from every nation under heaven. When they heard this sound, a crowd came together in bewilderment, because each one heard them speaking in his own language. Utterly amazed, they asked: "Are not all these men who are speaking Galileans? Then how is it that each of us hears them in his own native language? Parthians, Medes and Elamites; residents of Mesopotamia, Judea and Cappadocia, Pontus and Asia, Phrygia and Pamphylia, Egypt and the parts of Libya near Cyrene; visitors from Rome (both Jews and converts to Judaism); Cretans and Arabs—we hear them declaring the wonders of God in our own tongues!" Amazed and perplexed, they asked one another, "What does this mean?"

MEDITATE

In Genesis 11 we see the human race conspiring together to build a tower reaching to heaven to "make a name for ourselves." In response, God "came down," confused their language, and scattered them across the face of the earth. Now, note who is in the room on the day of Pentecost. The scattered are gathered, and God comes down, but the Spirit does not reorder the world by the restoration of a single language, he does it through the proclamation of one gospel, through the diversity of many languages.

It could have gone the other way. If the Spirit can cause uneducated men to speak in a multiplicity of foreign languages, he could have easily caused all the people to miraculously understand the message in a single language. Ponder the implications of this. What does this say about unity and diversity? What does this say about God's way of "loving the world?" What's the big idea here and what difference does it make in your own life?

REFLECT

If, then, the Holy Spirit is truly, and not in name only, called Divine both by Scripture and by our Fathers, what ground is left for those who oppose the glory of the Spirit? He is Divine, and absolutely good, and Omnipotent, and wise, and glorious, and eternal; He is everything of this kind that can be named to raise our thoughts to the grandeur of His being.

—From *On the Holy Spirit*
Gregory of Nyssa

ASK

Express your questions, doubts, curiosities, and conundrums.

AFFIRM

Write any fresh affirmation stirring in your heart and mind from today.

Now affirm the Apostles' Creed aloud:

I believe in God, the Father Almighty, creator of heaven and earth, I believe in Jesus Christ, His only Son, our Lord . . .

Day 3: *No Branch Can Bear Fruit by Itself*

READ

John 14:15–18; 25–27

"If you love me, you will obey what I command. And I will ask the Father, and he will give you another Counselor to be with you forever—the Spirit of truth. The world cannot accept him, because it neither sees him nor knows him. But you know him, for he lives with you and will be in you. I will not leave you as orphans; I will come to you."

"All this I have spoken while still with you. But the Counselor, the Holy Spirit, whom the Father will send in my name, will teach you all things and will remind you of everything I have said to you. Peace I leave with you; my peace I give you. I do not give to you as the world gives. Do not let your hearts be troubled and do not be afraid."

John 15:4

"Remain in me, and I will remain in you. No branch can bear fruit by itself; it must remain in the vine. Neither can you bear fruit unless you remain in me."

John 16:12–15

"I have much more to say to you, more than you can now bear. But when he, the Spirit of truth, comes, he will guide you into all truth. He will not speak on his own; he will speak only what he hears, and he will tell you what is yet to come. He will bring glory to me by taking from what is mine and making it known to you. All that belongs to the Father is mine. That is why I said the Spirit will take from what is mine and make it known to you."

MEDITATE

In John's Gospel, Jesus' last words to his disciples deal almost exclusively with the Holy Spirit. He tells them his secret. Earlier in the Gospel he describes his work by saying he says only what he hears the Father saying and does only what he sees the Father doing. The Father and the Son and the Holy Spirit work together in a profoundly bonded community and through an exquisitely unified order. In this revelatory teaching, Jesus prepares us to be brought on the inside of this community to participate in this order. This is extraordinary.

In fact, at the climax of Jesus' teaching he offers what is arguably the most substantive prayer that we have recorded (see John 17). He prays specifically for us, saying, "My prayer, Father, is that all of them would be one; just as you are in me and I am in you. May they also be in us so that the world may believe that you have sent me." What he asks for seems impossible; that our relationships with each other would have the very same character of union of his relationship with his Father. Further, he asks for our community to be brought inside of their community. Finally, he links all of this to the ability for the world to believe in him. Could this be why he focuses so much on the Holy Spirit in his final hours with the disciples? Think on these things.

To say, "I believe in the Holy Spirit," is not assent to a doctrinal concept but rather to open yourself to full participation in the ministry of the gospel and all its implications.

REFLECT

Breathe in me, O Holy Spirit, that my thoughts may all be holy.
Act in me, O Holy Spirit, that my work, too, may be holy.
Draw my heart, O Holy Spirit, that I love but what is holy.
Strengthen me, O Holy Spirit, to defend all that is holy.
Guard me, then, O Holy Spirit, that I always may be holy.
Amen.

—From *Prayer to the Holy Spirit*
St. Augustine of Hippo

ASK

Express your questions, doubts, curiosities, and conundrums.

AFFIRM

Write any fresh affirmation stirring in your heart and mind from today.

Now affirm the Apostles' Creed aloud:

*I believe in God, the Father Almighty, creator of heaven and earth, I believe
in Jesus Christ, His only Son, our Lord . . .*

Day 4: *So I Say, Walk by the Spirit*

READ

Galatians 5:16–18; 22–26

> *So I say, walk by the Spirit, and you will not gratify the desires of the flesh. For the flesh desires what is contrary to the Spirit, and the Spirit what is contrary to the flesh. They are in conflict with each other, so that you are not to do whatever you want. But if you are led by the Spirit, you are not under the law . . .*
>
> *But the fruit of the Spirit is love, joy, peace, forbearance, kindness, goodness, faithfulness, gentleness and self-control. Against such things there is no law. Those who belong to Christ Jesus have crucified the flesh with its passions and desires. Since we live by the Spirit, let us keep in step with the Spirit. Let us not become conceited, provoking and envying each other.*

MEDITATE

Have you come face-to-face with your utter inability to live the Christian life in your own strength and initiative? It's subtle how we try. We mistake imitation for immersion. While these are not mutually exclusive, to attempt the imitation of Christ apart from deep immersion in the Holy Spirit leads to futility and frustration. Are you ready to receive the fullness of the Holy Spirit? The life "led by the Spirit" requires deep immersion in the Spirit and continual filling. Remember the prayer, "Come Holy Spirit."

REFLECT

The Holy Spirit is the Spirit of life and light and love . . . Toward nature He performs one sort of work, toward the world another, and toward the Church still another. And every act of His accords with the will of the Triune God. Never does He act on impulse nor move after a quick or arbitrary decision. Since He is the Spirit of the Father He feels toward His people exactly as the Father feels, so there need be on our part no sense of strangeness in His presence. He will always act like Jesus, toward sinners in compassion, toward saints in warm affection, toward human suffering in tenderest pity and love.

—From *God's Pursuit of Man*
A. W. Tozer

ASK

Express your questions, doubts, curiosities, and conundrums.

AFFIRM

Write any fresh affirmation stirring in your heart and mind from today.

Now affirm the Apostles' Creed aloud:

I believe in God, the Father Almighty, creator of heaven and earth, I believe in Jesus Christ, His only Son, our Lord . . .

Day 5: *For the Common Good*

READ

1 Corinthians 12:7–14

> *Now to each one the manifestation of the Spirit is given for the common good. To one there is given through the Spirit a message of wisdom, to another a message of knowledge by means of the same Spirit, to another faith by the same Spirit, to another gifts of healing by that one Spirit, to another miraculous powers, to another prophecy, to another distinguishing between spirits, to another speaking in different kinds of tongues, and to still another the interpretation of tongues. All these are the work of one and the same Spirit, and he distributes them to each one, just as he determines.*
>
> *Just as a body, though one, has many parts, but all its many parts form one body, so it is with Christ. For we were all baptized by one Spirit so as to form one body— whether Jews or Gentiles, slave or free—and we were all given the one Spirit to drink. Even so the body is not made up of one part but of many.*

MEDITATE

Imagine a group of people brought together to a building site. Everything needed to build a house is there by way of supplies and materials. The only thing missing are the skills and the tools. No one in the group has any tools and none are trained home builders. (Additionally, no one has any money to purchase any tools.) They need someone to come along and provide the tools and the training on how to work together to build the house.

It is perhaps oversimplified, but this metaphor aptly describes how the Spirit of God works within human communities to build up the body of Christ. Everyone who receives the gift of the Holy Spirit receives gifts from the Holy Spirit. These gifts may not reflect our natural inclinations and proclivities or some particular "talent" of ours. The gifts of the Spirit are supernatural, grace-empowered abilities and skills. The body of Christ will not be built up without them.

Are you aware of the gift(s) of the Spirit that you've been given? Have you had any training to work with this gift?

REFLECT

There is no need for us to wait, as the one hundred and twenty had to wait [Acts 1], for the Spirit to come. For the Holy Spirit did come on the day of Pentecost, and has never left his church. Our responsibility is to humble ourselves before his sovereign authority, to determine not to quench him, but to allow him his freedom. For then our churches will again manifest those marks of the Spirit's presence which many young people are especially looking for, namely biblical teaching, loving fellowship, living worship, and an ongoing, outgoing evangelism.

—From *Authentic Christianity*
John R. W. Stott

ASK

Express your questions, doubts, curiosities, and conundrums.

AFFIRM

Write any fresh affirmation stirring in your heart and mind from today.

Now affirm the Apostles' Creed aloud:

> *I believe in God, the Father Almighty, creator of heaven and earth, I believe in Jesus Christ, His only Son, our Lord . . .*

Day 6: *But the Greatest of These Is Love*

READ

1 Corinthians 13:1–13

If I speak in the tongues of men or of angels, but do not have love, I am only a resounding gong or a clanging cymbal. If I have the gift of prophecy and can fathom all mysteries and all knowledge, and if I have a faith that can move mountains, but do not have love, I am nothing. If I give all I possess to the poor and give over my body to hardship that I may boast, but do not have love, I gain nothing.

Love is patient, love is kind. It does not envy, it does not boast, it is not proud. It does not dishonor others, it is not self-seeking, it is not easily angered, it keeps no record of wrongs. Love does not delight in evil but rejoices with the truth. It always protects, always trusts, always hopes, always perseveres.

Love never fails. But where there are prophecies, they will cease; where there are tongues, they will be stilled; where there is knowledge, it will pass away. For we know in part and we prophesy in part, but when completeness comes, what is in part disappears. When I was a child, I talked like a child, I thought like a child, I reasoned like a child. When I became a man, I put the ways of childhood behind me. For now we see only a reflection as in a mirror; then we shall see face to face. Now I know in part; then I shall know fully, even as I am fully known.

And now these three remain: faith, hope and love. But the greatest of these is love.

MEDITATE

The bottom-line evidence of the Spirit's presence in your life is not the gifts of the Spirit, but the love of God. In at least two places in Scripture we see the gifts enumerated and immediately followed by the call to love. The text above emphatically declares anything we do by way of the gifts of the Spirit without love amounts to nothing. The Holy Spirit enables and empowers supernatural, divine love to work in and through human beings.

Dwell on this passage from 2 Peter 1:3–4: "His divine power has given us everything we need for life and godliness through our knowledge of him who called us by his own glory and goodness. Through these he has given us his very great and precious promises, so that through them you may participate in the divine nature and escape the corruption in the world caused by evil desires."

Where do you find yourself on the continuum below? What would help you move to the right?

Corrupted by sin————————————————————Participating in
the Divine Nature

REFLECT

If we think of the Holy Spirit as so many do as merely a power or influence, our constant thought will be, "How can I get more of the Holy Spirit," but if we think of Him in the biblical way as a Divine Person, our thought will rather be, "How can the Holy Spirit have more of me?"

—From *The Person and Work of the Holy Spirit*
R. A. Torrey

ASK

Express your questions, doubts, curiosities, and conundrums.

AFFIRM

Write any fresh affirmation stirring in your heart and mind from today.

Now affirm the Apostles' Creed aloud:

I believe in God, the Father Almighty, creator of heaven and earth, I believe in Jesus Christ, His only Son, our Lord . . .

Week 6

The Holy Catholic Church, the Communion of Saints

Day I: *I Will Build My Church*

READ

Matthew 16:13–20

> *When Jesus came to the region of Caesarea Philippi, he asked his disciples, "Who do people say the Son of Man is?"*
>
> *They replied, "Some say John the Baptist; others say Elijah; and still others, Jeremiah or one of the prophets."*
>
> *"But what about you?" he asked. "Who do you say I am?"*
>
> *Simon Peter answered, "You are the Messiah, the Son of the living God."*
>
> *Jesus replied, "Blessed are you, Simon son of Jonah, for this was not revealed to you by flesh and blood, but by my Father in heaven. And I tell you that you are Peter, and on this rock I will build my church, and the gates of Hades will not overcome it. I will give you the keys of the kingdom of heaven; whatever you bind on earth will be bound in heaven, and whatever you loose on earth will be loosed in heaven." Then he ordered his disciples not to tell anyone that he was the Messiah.*

MEDITATE

It was the question of the first century. It is the question of the twenty-first century. And it's been the question for every century in between. "Who do you say I am?"

There is a "right" answer, as in, "You are the Christ, the Son of the Living God." Then there is a *revealed* response. Anyone can mimic the "answer," but only the Spirit can reveal the response. Paul says a similar thing to the Corinthian Church when he said, "Therefore I tell you that no one who is speaking by the Spirit of God says, 'Jesus be cursed,' and no one can say, 'Jesus is Lord,' except by the Holy Spirit" (1 Cor. 12:3).

It's too easy to settle for the "right" Sunday school answer to this question. Are you responding to the question from a deeper place; a place where you know that you know that you know who Jesus is and who Jesus is to you?

Too often we seem willing to build our Church on right answers and checked boxes. Jesus builds his Church on true confessions, revealed responses. Against the cumulative power of such a response, the gates of Hades cannot prevail.

When we declare, "I believe in the holy catholic Church," we take stock in the Church Jesus is building.

REFLECT

Without Christ there is discord between God and man and between man and man. Christ become the Mediator and made peace with God and among men. Without Christ we should not know God, we could not call upon him, nor come to him. But without Christ we also could not know our brother, nor could we come to him. The way is blocked by our own ego. Christ opened the way to God and our brother. Now Christians can live with one another in peace; they can become one. But they can continue to do so only by way of Jesus Christ, only in Christ Jesus are we one, only through Jesus Christ are we bound together. To eternity He remains one Mediator.

—From *Life Together*
Dietrich Bonhoeffer

ASK

Express your questions, doubts, curiosities, and conundrums.

AFFIRM

Write any fresh affirmation stirring in your heart and mind from today.

Now affirm the Apostles' Creed aloud:

I believe in God, the Father Almighty, creator of heaven and earth, I believe in Jesus Christ, His only Son, our Lord . . .

Day 2: *A People Belonging to God*

READ
1 Peter 2:1–12

Therefore, rid yourselves of all malice and all deceit, hypocrisy, envy, and slander of every kind. Like newborn babies, crave pure spiritual milk, so that by it you may grow up in your salvation, now that you have tasted that the Lord is good.

As you come to him, the living Stone—rejected by men but chosen by God and precious to him—you also, like living stones, are being built into a spiritual house to be a holy priesthood, offering spiritual sacrifices acceptable to God through Jesus Christ. For in Scripture it says:

"See, I lay a stone in Zion, a chosen and precious cornerstone, and the one who trusts in him will never be put to shame."

Now to you who believe, this stone is precious. But to those who do not believe,

"The stone the builders rejected has become the capstone," and,

"A stone that causes men to stumble and a rock that makes them fall."

They stumble because they disobey the message—which is also what they were destined for.

But you are a chosen people, a royal priesthood, a holy nation, a people belonging to God, that you may declare the praises of him who called you out of darkness into his wonderful light. Once you were not a people, but now you are the people of God; once you had not received mercy, but now you have received mercy.

Dear friends, I urge you, as aliens and strangers in the world, to abstain from sinful desires, which war against your soul. Live such good lives among the pagans that, though they accuse you of doing wrong, they may see your good deeds and glorify God on the day he visits us.

MEDITATE

Note how this passage begins and ends with exhortations about holiness. When the Creed modifies the word "Church" with "holy," it means this church is distinctive in character. When Peter tells us we are "aliens and strangers" in the world he doesn't mean we need to be strange or alienate people. He means we are set apart. There is something about our character and presence that is wholesomely winsome. He urges us to grow up in our salvation, to press on to mature faith. Reflect a bit on this call to "crave pure spiritual milk." What would that be? Why do we find ourselves in the position of approaching holiness more like taking medicine than craving pure milk? So often the people of God take a wrong turn when it comes to holiness, making it all about duty and discipline. True holiness is all about desire and delight. It is about tasting the goodness of God. What would it be like to "crave" the Spirit of God? How could that happen?

Peter is not talking about the holiness that comes from the Pharisaic model with its meticulous observance of legal codes. When he says holiness, he means Jesus, the cornerstone.

REFLECT

Saints cannot exist without a community, as they require, like all of us, nurturance by a people who, while often unfaithful, preserve the habits necessary to learn the story of God.

—From "The Gesture of a Truthful Story"
Stanley Hauerwas

ASK

Express your questions, doubts, curiosities, and conundrums.

AFFIRM

Write any fresh affirmation stirring in your heart and mind from today.

Now affirm the Apostles' Creed aloud:

I believe in God, the Father Almighty, creator of heaven and earth, I believe in Jesus Christ, His only Son, our Lord . . .

Day 3: *It Seemed Good to the Holy Spirit and to Us*

READ

Acts 15: 22–35

Then the apostles and elders, with the whole church, decided to choose some of their own men and send them to Antioch with Paul and Barnabas. They chose Judas (called Barsabbas) and Silas, two men who were leaders among the brothers. With them they sent the following letter:

The apostles and elders, your brothers,

To the Gentile believers in Antioch, Syria and Cilicia:

Greetings.

We have heard that some went out from us without our authorization and disturbed you, troubling your minds by what they said. So we all agreed to choose some men and send them to you with our dear friends Barnabas and Paul—men who have risked their lives for the name of our Lord Jesus Christ. Therefore we are sending Judas and Silas to confirm by word of mouth what we are writing. It seemed good to the Holy Spirit and to us not to burden you with anything beyond the following requirements: You are to abstain from food sacrificed to idols, from blood, from the meat of strangled animals and from sexual immorality. You will do well to avoid these things.

Farewell.

The men were sent off and went down to Antioch, where they gathered the church together and delivered the letter. The people read it and were glad for its encouraging message. Judas and Silas, who themselves were prophets, said much to encourage and strengthen the brothers. After spending some time there, they were sent off by the brothers with the blessing of peace to return to those who had sent them. But Paul and Barnabas remained in Antioch, where they and many others taught and preached the word of the Lord.

MEDITATE

The other identifier in the Creed is the word "catholic." This does not mean Roman Catholic. It means whole or universal. To say we believe in "the holy catholic Church" means we believe the Church of Jesus Christ is fundamentally one church in its essence. In the text above, we witness a potentially massive divide get mended through apostolic wisdom. Their decision not to require circumcision of the Gentiles paved the way for the body of Christ to develop as a universal fellowship.

The ecumenical creeds (Apostles and Nicene) play an essential role in preserving the catholicity of the Church. The creeds define the center of the Christian faith, the place of agreement and unity among all Christians in all times at all places. At the same time, the creeds outline the circumference, or boundaries, of the faith. It creates a generous space where a lot of doctrinal distinctions can be carved out and around which there may be significant disagreement. Wesley's followers have long employed the phrase, "In essentials, unity; in non-essentials, liberty; and in all things, charity," with respect to the Church and particularly as it related to the Methodist movement.

REFLECT

I appeal to you, brothers and sisters, in the name of our Lord Jesus Christ, that all of you agree with one another in what you say and that there be no divisions among you, but that you be perfectly united in mind and thought.

—1 Corinthians 1:10

ASK

Express your questions, doubts, curiosities, and conundrums.

AFFIRM

Write any fresh affirmation stirring in your heart and mind from today.

Now affirm the Apostles' Creed aloud:

I believe in God, the Father Almighty, creator of heaven and earth, I believe in Jesus Christ, His only Son, our Lord . . .

Day 4: *You Are All One in Christ Jesus*

READ

Galatians 3:26–29

You are all sons of God through faith in Christ Jesus, for all of you who were baptized into Christ have clothed yourselves with Christ. There is neither Jew nor Greek, slave nor free, male nor female, for you are all one in Christ Jesus. If you belong to Christ, then you are Abraham's seed, and heirs according to the promise.

Colossians 3:5–11

Put to death, therefore, whatever belongs to your earthly nature: sexual immorality, impurity, lust, evil desires and greed, which is idolatry. Because of these, the wrath of God is coming. You used to walk in these ways, in the life you once lived. But now you must rid yourselves of all such things as these: anger, rage, malice, slander, and filthy language from your lips. Do not lie to each other, since you have taken off your old self with its practices and have put on the new self, which is being renewed in knowledge in the image of its Creator. Here there is no Greek or Jew, circumcised or uncircumcised, barbarian, Scythian, slave or free, but Christ is all, and is in all.

MEDITATE

The unity given to the people of God in Jesus Christ exceeds the disunity which originates from gender differences, ethnicity, religious observance, and social status. The Church is the place where this unity is given yet at the same time has to be worked into. This new-creation reality is declared and celebrated in baptism. It must be claimed and enacted in everyday life. The imagery given is one of changing clothes; putting off the clothes of the old self and putting on the clothes of the new self, which is Christ. In affirming our faith in the holiness and catholicity of the Church, we, in a sense, all put on identical clothing. The Creed intends to unite us in the essential, which is Christ. This brings to mind the imagery of the multitudes of diverse peoples gathered around the Lamb who are all wearing white robes (Rev. 7:9). Meditate on these things.

REFLECT

Here in the church there is the one thing needful: Here is a refuge from the vanity and the storms of life. Here is the calm harbor for souls seeking after salvation. Here is incorruptible food and drink for the soul. Here is the light that enlightens all men existing upon earth. Here is the clean air of the spirit. Here is the fountain of living water which flows to life eternal (John 4:14). Here are distributed the gifts of the Holy Spirit, here is the cleansing of souls.

—From "On Prayer in Church"
St. John of Kronstadt

ASK

Express your questions, doubts, curiosities, and conundrums.

AFFIRM

Write any fresh affirmation stirring in your heart and mind from today.

Now affirm the Apostles' Creed aloud:

I believe in God, the Father Almighty, creator of heaven and earth, I believe in Jesus Christ, His only Son, our Lord . . .

Day 5: *A Great Multitude No One Could Count*

READ

Revelation 7:9–12

> *After this I looked and there before me was a great multitude that no one could count, from every nation, tribe, people and language, standing before the throne and in front of the Lamb. They were wearing white robes and were holding palm branches in their hands. And they cried out in a loud voice:*
>
> *"Salvation belongs to our God, who sits on the throne, and to the Lamb."*
>
> *All the angels were standing around the throne and around the elders and the four living creatures. They fell down on their faces before the throne and worshiped God, saying:*
>
> *"Amen! Praise and glory and wisdom and thanks and honor and power and strength be to our God for ever and ever. Amen!"*

MEDITATE

In this text we are given a glimpse of ultimate reality, the great communion of saints gathered for worship. Invite the Spirit of God to grant you a holy imagination. Picture the scene: People from every nation, tribe, people, and language in numbers impossible to count, though they all look different they all wear the same white robes and they all hold palm branches, and at the center of this gathering is a single Lamb. All the people cry out, "Amen! Praise and glory and wisdom and thanks and honor and power and strength be to our God for ever and ever. Amen!"

Take a few minutes and slowly copy those words of adulation on the paper below. Now recite it aloud several times, growing in intensity with each time. As you declare these words, become conscious of the way your spirit is worshipping God.

REFLECT

Head of Thy church, whose Spirit fills
And flows through every faithful soul,
Unites in mystic love, and seals
Them one, and sanctifies the whole;

"Come, Lord," Thy glorious Spirit cries,
And souls beneath the altar groan;
"Come, Lord," the bride on earth replies,
"And perfect all our souls in one."

—From "Head of Thy Church, Whose Spirit Fills"
Charles Wesley

ASK

Express your questions, doubts, curiosities, and conundrums.

AFFIRM

Write any fresh affirmation stirring in your heart and mind from today.

Now affirm the Apostles' Creed aloud:

I believe in God, the Father Almighty, creator of heaven and earth, I believe in Jesus Christ, His only Son, our Lord . . .

Day 6: *Let Us Run with Perseverance*

READ

Hebrews 12:1–3; 18–24

> *Therefore, since we are surrounded by such a great cloud of witnesses, let us throw off everything that hinders and the sin that so easily entangles, and let us run with perseverance the race marked out for us. Let us fix our eyes on Jesus, the author and perfecter of our faith, who for the joy set before him endured the cross, scorning its shame, and sat down at the right hand of the throne of God. Consider him who endured such opposition from sinful men, so that you will not grow weary and lose heart. . . .*
>
> *You have not come to a mountain that can be touched and that is burning with fire; to darkness, gloom and storm; to a trumpet blast or to such a voice speaking words that those who heard it begged that no further word be spoken to them, because they could not bear what was commanded: "If even an animal touches the mountain, it must be stoned." The sight was so terrifying that Moses said, "I am trembling with fear."*
>
> *But you have come to Mount Zion, to the heavenly Jerusalem, the city of the living God. You have come to thousands upon thousands of angels in joyful assembly, to the church of the firstborn, whose names are written in heaven. You have come to God, the judge of all men, to the spirits of righteous men made perfect, to Jesus the mediator of a new covenant, and to the sprinkled blood that speaks a better word than the blood of Abel.*

MEDITATE

Sin is an entanglement. Holiness is a vision. Could it be that entanglements and encumbrances snare us at the point where we lose our vision of the bigger picture? We were made to run in the pathway of holiness, to live lives of captivating beauty which inspire the awe of God.

Perhaps this is why the Bible constantly casts vision of the good life. Note the pattern. Become aware of the "great cloud of witnesses," or the communion of saints. From the encouragement of such a great assembly, cast sin aside and extricate yourself from its encumbrance. Now refocus your gaze on Jesus Christ, the Alpha and Omega of it all.

Are you entangled with some particular sin? Are you encumbered with discouragement or despair? Remember the creed: "I believe in Jesus Christ, his only Son, our Lord." Run to him. Locate yourself on the continuum below. Consider how you might move further to the right.

Encumbered————————————————————————Running with
and Entangled   Perseverance

REFLECT

They verily are not the true congregation of Christ who merely boast of his name. But they are the true congregation of Christ who are truly converted, who are born from above of God, who are of a regenerate mind by the operation of the Holy Spirit through the hearing of the divine Word, and have become the children of God, have entered into obedience to him, and live unblamably in his holy commandments, and according to his holy will with all their days, or from the moment of their call.

—From "Why I Do Not Cease Teaching and Writing"
Menno Simons

ASK

Express your questions, doubts, curiosities, and conundrums.

AFFIRM

Write any fresh affirmation stirring in your heart and mind from today.

Now affirm the Apostles' Creed aloud:

I believe in God, the Father Almighty, creator of heaven and earth, I believe in Jesus Christ, His only Son, our Lord . . .

Week 7

The Forgiveness of Sins, the Resurrection of the Body, and the Life Everlasting

READ

Hebrews 10:1–14

> *The law is only a shadow of the good things that are coming—not the realities themselves. For this reason it can never, by the same sacrifices repeated endlessly year after year, make perfect those who draw near to worship. Otherwise, would they not have stopped being offered? For the worshipers would have been cleansed once for all, and would no longer have felt guilty for their sins. But those sacrifices are an annual reminder of sins. It is impossible for the blood of bulls and goats to take away sins.*
>
> *Therefore, when Christ came into the world, he said:*
>
> *"Sacrifice and offering you did not desire, but a body you prepared for me; with burnt offerings and sin offerings you were not pleased. Then I said, 'Here I am—it is written about me in the scroll—I have come to do your will, my God.'"*
>
> *First he said, "Sacrifices and offerings, burnt offerings and sin offerings you did not desire, nor were you pleased with them"—though they were offered in accordance with the law. Then he said, "Here I am, I have come to do your will." He sets aside*

the first to establish the second. And by that will, we have been made holy through the sacrifice of the body of Jesus Christ once for all.

Day after day every priest stands and performs his religious duties; again and again he offers the same sacrifices, which can never take away sins. **But when this priest had offered for all time one sacrifice for sins, he sat down at the right hand of God, and since that time he waits for his enemies to be made his footstool. For by one sacrifice he has made perfect forever those who are being made holy.**

MEDITATE

These last several phrases of the Creed can be flown through all too easily. By this point, we find ourselves reciting the words with a kind of cadence. It will be important to break our stride to take stock of the magnitude of what we are affirming.

"I believe in . . . the forgiveness of sins." Wait! Isn't this at the very core of the gospel? On May 24, 1738, John Wesley penned these words in his journal:

> In the evening I went very unwillingly to a society in Aldersgate Street, where one was reading Luther's preface to the Epistle to the Romans. About a quarter before nine, while the leader was describing the change which God works in the heart through faith in Christ, I felt my heart strangely warmed. I felt I did trust in Christ alone for salvation; and an assurance was given me that He had taken away *my* sins, even *mine*, and saved *me* from the law of sin and death.

The forgiveness of sins cannot remain a propositional concept to which we give mental assent. It must be an experienced reality. Do you have an inner assurance that your sins have been forgiven? Do you believe there are sins in your past that cannot be forgiven? Are you struggling with an entangling sin for which you don't feel you can continue to ask for forgiveness? Are you struggling to forgive yourself for some sin in your past?

To believe in the forgiveness of sins means we have to confront these roadblocks with the unstoppable grace of God. Identify the place of stuckness and present this to God, standing on the finished work of Christ. If you have enjoyed an experience of God's forgiveness and the deep assurance of grace, write about it. Tell the story in your journal. This is your testimony and it holds the power to bless others.

REFLECT

What can wash away my sin?
Nothing but the blood of Jesus;
What can make me whole again?
Nothing but the blood of Jesus.

Oh! precious is the flow
That makes me white as snow;
No other fount I know,
Nothing but the blood of Jesus.

For my pardon, this I see,
Nothing but the blood of Jesus;
For my cleansing this my plea,
Nothing but the blood of Jesus.

Nothing can for sin atone,
Nothing but the blood of Jesus;
Naught of good that I have done,
Nothing but the blood of Jesus.

This is all my hope and peace,
Nothing but the blood of Jesus;
This is all my righteousness,
Nothing but the blood of Jesus.

Now by this I'll overcome—
Nothing but the blood of Jesus,
Now by this I'll reach my home—
Nothing but the blood of Jesus.

Glory! Glory! This I sing—
Nothing but the blood of Jesus,
All my praise for this I bring—
Nothing but the blood of Jesus.

—"Nothing But the Blood"
Robert Lowry

ASK

Express your questions, doubts, curiosities, and conundrums.

AFFIRM

Write any fresh affirmation stirring in your heart and mind from today.

Now affirm the Apostles' Creed aloud:

I believe in God, the Father Almighty, creator of heaven and earth, I believe in Jesus Christ, His only Son, our Lord . . .

Day 2: *As We Also Have Forgiven Our Debtors*

READ

Matthew 6:9–15

> *This, then, is how you should pray:*
> *"Our Father in heaven, hallowed be your name, your kingdom come, your will be done on earth as it is in heaven. Give us today our daily bread. Forgive us our debts, as we also have forgiven our debtors. And lead us not into temptation, but deliver us from the evil one."*
> *For if you forgive men when they sin against you, your heavenly Father will also forgive you. But if you do not forgive men their sins, your Father will not forgive your sins.*

MEDITATE

In the prayer he taught us, Jesus embeds a stern warning concerning the forgiveness of sins. He goes so far as to make explicit commentary on this phrase after he ends the prayer. The bottom line: If we do not forgive others, we will not be forgiven. Have you really considered the magnitude of this warning? Our un-forgiveness is the only barrier to our being forgiven. Dwell with this thought today. It has been said that un-forgiveness is to drink poison while expecting it to kill the other person. It only destroys you.

Are you withholding forgiveness in some relationship in your life or from your past? It is urgent for you to re-approach forgiveness. Keep in mind that forgiveness does not mean reconciliation with everything going back to normal. In its most basic form, forgiveness is the willful decision to cease retaliating against the other person, either inwardly or outwardly.

REFLECT

Let none lament his failings, forgiveness has risen from the tomb. Let none fear death, for the death of the Savior has set us free.

—From "Easter Sermon"
John Chrysostom

ASK

Express your questions, doubts, curiosities, and conundrums.

AFFIRM

Write any fresh affirmation stirring in your heart and mind from today.

Now affirm the Apostles' Creed aloud:

> *I believe in God, the Father Almighty, creator of heaven and earth, I believe in Jesus Christ, His only Son, our Lord . . .*

Day 3: *Then the End Will Come*

READ

1 Corinthians 15:12–28

But if it is preached that Christ has been raised from the dead, how can some of you say that there is no resurrection of the dead? If there is no resurrection of the dead, then not even Christ has been raised. And if Christ has not been raised, our preaching is useless and so is your faith. More than that, we are then found to be false witnesses about God, for we have testified about God that he raised Christ from the dead. But he did not raise him if in fact the dead are not raised. For if the dead are not raised, then Christ has not been raised either. And if Christ has not been raised, your faith is futile; you are still in your sins. Then those also who have fallen asleep in Christ are lost. If only for this life we have hope in Christ, we are of all people most to be pitied.

But Christ has indeed been raised from the dead, the firstfruits of those who have fallen asleep. For since death came through a man, the resurrection of the dead comes also through a man. For as in Adam all die, so in Christ all will be made alive. But each in turn: Christ, the firstfruits; then, when he comes, those who belong to him. Then the end will come, when he hands over the kingdom to God the Father after he has destroyed all dominion, authority and power. For he must reign until he has put all his enemies under his feet. The last enemy to be destroyed is death. For he "has put everything under his feet." Now when it says that "everything" has been put under him, it is clear that this does not include God himself, who put everything under Christ. When he has done this, then the Son himself will be made subject to him who put everything under him, so that God may be all in all.

MEDITATE

In this passage Paul draws from apostolic logic to persuade his readers of the uncompromisable essential of the "resurrection of the dead" to the faith of a follower of Jesus. He goes so far to say that if there is no ultimate resurrection of the dead, then Christ was not raised from the dead. In an interesting way he seems to say history depends on the future. He can't make it any more clear: If the resurrection from the dead is not true, then all bets are off. We have wasted our time. Ponder that. Perhaps this is why the Creed makes such explicit reference, "I believe in . . . the resurrection of the body."

So here's the question: Does the bodily resurrection from the dead figure prominently in your own faith? Can you stand with Paul in this logic?

REFLECT

Christ is risen from the dead, rise ye with Him. Christ is returned again to Himself, return ye. Christ is freed from the tomb, be ye freed from the bond of sin. The gates of hell are opened, and death is destroyed, and the old Adam is put aside, and the New is fulfilled; if any man be in Christ he is a new creature; be ye renewed.

—From *Oration XLV*
Gregory Nazianzen

ASK

Express your questions, doubts, curiosities, and conundrums.

AFFIRM

Write any fresh affirmation stirring in your heart and mind from today.

Now affirm the Apostles' Creed aloud:

I believe in God, the Father Almighty, creator of heaven and earth, I believe in Jesus Christ, His only Son, our Lord . . .

Day 4: *Sown In Weakness—Raised In Power*

READ

1 Corinthians 15:35–49

But someone will ask, "How are the dead raised? With what kind of body will they come?" How foolish! What you sow does not come to life unless it dies. When you sow, you do not plant the body that will be, but just a seed, perhaps of wheat or of something else. But God gives it a body as he has determined, and to each kind of seed he gives its own body. Not all flesh is the same: People have one kind of flesh, animals have another, birds another and fish another. There are also heavenly bodies and there are earthly bodies; but the splendor of the heavenly bodies is one kind, and the splendor of the earthly bodies is another. The sun has one kind of splendor, the moon another and the stars another; and star differs from star in splendor.

So will it be with the resurrection of the dead. The body that is sown is perishable, it is raised imperishable; it is sown in dishonor, it is raised in glory; it is sown in weakness, it is raised in power; it is sown a natural body, it is raised a spiritual body.

If there is a natural body, there is also a spiritual body. So it is written: "The first man Adam became a living being"; the last Adam, a life-giving spirit. The spiritual did not come first, but the natural, and after that the spiritual. The first man was of the dust of the earth; the second man is of heaven. As was the earthly man, so are those who are of the earth; and as is the heavenly man, so also are those who are of heaven. And just as we have borne the image of the earthly man, so shall we bear the image of the heavenly man.

MEDITATE

The resurrection of the dead has tremendous implications for the living. We cannot live as though Creation does not matter. When it comes to the end of time, Scripture makes a few things somewhat clear. Heaven will not be some ethereal existence "up there." Heaven comes down and ushers in a New Creation. There will be continuity with the old creation and yet there will be discontinuity. The same is true with respect to our bodies. The mystery is what aspect of our created self continues and what is discontinued. Does knowing there will be elements of continuation with your present body in the New Creation change your perspective on your physical body here and now? How?

REFLECT

But you do not believe that the dead are raised. When the resurrection shall take place, then you will believe, whether you will or no; and your faith shall be reckoned for unbelief, unless you believe now . . . Moreover, you believe that the images made by men are gods, and do great things; and can you not believe that the God who made you is able also to make you afterwards?

—From a letter to Autolycus
Theophilus of Antioch

ASK

Express your questions, doubts, curiosities, and conundrums.

AFFIRM

Write any fresh affirmation stirring in your heart and mind from today.

Now affirm the Apostles' Creed aloud:

I believe in God, the Father Almighty, creator of heaven and earth, I believe in Jesus Christ, His only Son, our Lord . . .

Day 5: *Now This Is Eternal Life*

READ

John 3:16–18

> *For God so loved the world that he gave his one and only Son, that whoever believes in him shall not perish but have eternal life. For God did not send his Son into the world to condemn the world, but to save the world through him. Whoever believes in him is not condemned, but whoever does not believe stands condemned already because they have not believed in the name of God's one and only Son.*

John 17:1–5

> *After Jesus said this, he looked toward heaven and prayed: "Father, the hour has come. Glorify your Son, that your Son may glorify you. For you granted him authority over all people that he might give eternal life to all those you have given him. Now this is eternal life: that they know you, the only true God, and Jesus Christ, whom you have sent. I have brought you glory on earth by finishing the work you gave me to do. And now, Father, glorify me in your presence with the glory I had with you before the world began."*

MEDITATE

Do you believe in everlasting life? If so, when does it begin? Is this something that happens after death? Scripture seems to say that eternal or everlasting life begins when you begin to know God. The Creed masterfully ends in keeping with the way it began. "I believe in God, the Father Almighty, creator of heaven and earth, I believe in Jesus Christ, His only Son, our Lord." Everlasting life begins with faith in God. If we can affirm the first claim of the Creed, we have already affirmed the final one.

We must be clear, though, about the concept of believing. On the one hand, believing cannot be reduced to mental assent to propositional assertions. Neither can belief find its moorings in the knowledge of scientific certainty, valuable as it may be. Nor does biblical faith require a turning away from knowledge and scientific inquiry. To believe, in the biblical sense, means to know something beyond the plane of knowledge. Belief is Holy Spirit-empowered inner confidence in the truth of a person. It comes as a gift from God and is given to those who seek it.

Are you waiting on something to happen before you believe? Or are you actively asking, seeking, and knocking in pursuit of the gift of faith? In the world's eyes, seeing is believing. In the Kingdom of God, believing is seeing. This is why we walk by faith and not by sight. Where do you find yourself in this process?

REFLECT

This eternal life then commences when it pleases the Father to reveal his Son in our hearts; when we first know Christ, being enabled "to call him Lord by the Holy Ghost;" when we can testify, our conscience bearing us witness in the Holy Ghost, "the life which I now live, I live by faith in the Son of God, who loved me, and gave himself for me." And then it is that happiness begins; happiness real, solid, substantial. Then it is that heaven is opened in the soul, that the proper, heavenly state commences, while the love of God, as loving us, is shed abroad in the heart, instantly producing love to all mankind; general, pure benevolence, together with its genuine fruits, lowliness, meekness, patience, contentedness in every state; an entire, clear, full acquiescence in the whole will of God; enabling us to "rejoice evermore, and in everything to give thanks."

—From "Sermon #77 on Spiritual Worship"
John Wesley

ASK
Express your questions, doubts, curiosities, and conundrums.

AFFIRM
Write any fresh affirmation stirring in your heart and mind from today.

Now affirm the Apostles' Creed aloud:

I believe in God, the Father Almighty, creator of heaven and earth, I believe in Jesus Christ, His only Son, our Lord . . .

Day 6: *I Am Making Everything New*

READ

Revelation 21:1–5

> *Then I saw "a new heaven and a new earth," for the first heaven and the first earth had passed away, and there was no longer any sea. I saw the Holy City, the new Jerusalem, coming down out of heaven from God, prepared as a bride beautifully dressed for her husband. And I heard a loud voice from the throne saying, "Now the dwelling of God is with men, and he will live with them. They will be his people, and God himself will be with them and be their God. He will wipe every tear from their eyes. There will be no more death or mourning or crying or pain, for the old order of things has passed away."*
>
> *He who was seated on the throne said, "I am making everything new!" Then he said, "Write this down, for these words are trustworthy and true."*

MEDITATE

The Bible closes as it begins, with a vision of New Creation. This is perhaps the largest framework for the whole of Scripture, from Creation to New Creation. Read this passage aloud. When finished, close your eyes and invite the Holy Spirit to give you the imagination to envision such a reality. No more death, mourning, crying, or pain. No more tears. This is not pie-in-the-sky. This is what we believe. How might our life change and our faith grow if we spent time every day imagining this promised future? How about we give it a shot?

REFLECT

But the most glorious of all will be the change which then will take place on the poor, sinful, miserable children of men. These had fallen in many respects, as from a greater height, so into a lower depth, than any other part of the creation. But they shall "hear a great voice out of heaven, saying, 'Behold, the tabernacle of God is with men: And he will dwell with them, and they shall be his people, and God himself shall be their God'" (Rev. 21:3–4). Hence will arise an unmixed state of holiness and happiness far superior to that which Adam enjoyed in Paradise. In how beautiful a manner is this described by the Apostle: "God shall wipe away all tears from their eyes; and there shall be no more death, neither sorrow, nor crying, neither shall there be any more pain: For the former things are done away!" As there will be no more death, and no more pain or sickness preparatory thereto; as there will be no more grieving for, or parting with, friends; so there will be no more sorrow or crying. Nay, but there will be a greater deliverance than all this; for there will be no more sin. And, to crown all, there will be a deep, an intimate, an uninterrupted union with God; a constant communion with the Father and his Son Jesus Christ, through the Spirit; a continual enjoyment of the Three-One God, and of all the creatures in him!

—From "Sermon #64 on The New Creation"
John Wesley

ASK

Express your questions, doubts, curiosities, and conundrums.

AFFIRM

Write any fresh affirmation stirring in your heart and mind from today.

Now affirm the Apostles' Creed aloud:

I believe in God, the Father Almighty, creator of heaven and earth, I believe in Jesus Christ, His only Son, our Lord . . .

About the Author

John David "J. D." Walt serves as the sower-in-chief for Seedbed, an online electronic and print publishing platform whose sole ambition is to "sow for a great awakening," by developing theological and ministry training resources for the local church. A sought-after speaker and conference leader, a published author and songwriter, J. D. has served as mentor to dozens of pastors and worship leaders around the world both well-known and unknown. He has also served as a pastor and teacher in the Passion movement and with Worship Central, the worship equipping ministry of Tim Hughes and Al Gordon of the United Kingdom. A 1997 graduate of Asbury Theological Seminary, J. D. writes regularly online at www.jdwalt.com. He is a licensed attorney in Arkansas and an ordained elder in the Texas Conference of the United Methodist Church. Follow him on twitter @jdwalt. He hails from Dumas, Arkansas, and is married to Tiffani, also an Asbury Seminary graduate. They reside on the Walt Farm in Wilmore, Kentucky, with their four children David, Mary Kathryn, Lily, and Samuel.